T0368102

VORGRIFF

Apprehending
the
Non-existent
God

PHILIP KRILL

authorHOUSE

AuthorHouse™
1663 Liberty Drive
Bloomington, IN 47403
www.authorhouse.com
Phone: 833-262-8899

Published by AuthorHouse   11/30/2024

ISBN: 979-8-8230-3858-4 (sc)
ISBN: 979-8-8230-3857-7 (e)

For

Michael J. Buckley, S.J.

In Memoriam

God is an utter Nothingness
Beyond the touch of time and place
The more you grasp after Him
The more He flees from your embrace.

Angelus Silesius, *The Cherubic Wanderer*

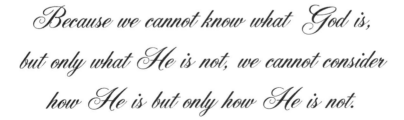

Because we cannot know what God is,
but only what He is not, we cannot consider
how He is but only how He is not.

St. Thomas Aquinas, *Summa Theologica*

CONTENTS

INTRODUCTION

I am indebted to two, great, mystical thinkers for inspiring the title, content, and structure of this book.

The *title* (*Vorgriff*) and *content* are borrowed from theologian **Karl Rahner**, who contends that 'the apprehension of every finite object transpires, as a condition of its possibility, before an infinite backdrop, or *excessus*, that, operating like a luminous silhouette, establishes the human subject in an implicit position of absolute openness to being in general'. For Rahner, the *Vorgriff* 'is the light by which everything else is seen, the always receding horizon that can never be directly examined, and the limitless whither whose desirability incites a dynamism in the subject impelling her beyond all finitude toward infinite *esse* - and thus, however implicitly, God'.[1] Though 'conscious', our *Vorgriff* is pre-conceptual, i.e. nonobjective and unthematic. It can never be adequately articulated, yet all a posteriori knowledge is an explication and thematization of this primordial apprehension. What I have written here is a much less erudite attempt than that of Rahner's to give expression to what I also believe can only be 'known' intuitively within a *Vorgriff* of God.

The *structure* of this book is one inspired by the later work of **Ludwig Wittgenstein,** who famously remarked, 'Whereof one cannot speak, thereof one must be silent'.[2] Feeling nevertheless

---

[1] Henry Shea. 'Internal Difficulties in the Theology of Karl Rahner', *Modern Theology*, vol. 37, no. 3.

[2] *Tractatus Logico-Philosophicus*

compelled to articulate his intuitions about how to speak about that which cannot be spoken about, Wittgenstein wrote: 'I have written down all these thoughts as remarks, short paragraphs, of which there is sometimes a fairly long chain about the same subject, while I sometimes make a sudden change, jumping from one topic to another. It was my intention at first to bring all this together in a book whose form I pictured differently...[b]ut the essential thing was that the thoughts should proceed from one subject to another in a natural order and without breaks. After several unsuccessful attempts to weld my results together into such a whole, I realized that I should never succeed. The best that I could write would never be more than philosophical remarks; my thoughts were soon crippled if I tried to force them on in any single direction against their natural inclination ... [thus] the philosophical remarks in this book are, as it were, a number of sketches of landscapes which were made in the course of these long and involved journeyings. The same or almost the same points were always being approached afresh from different directions, and new sketches made. Very many of these were badly drawn or uncharacteristic, marked by all the defects of a weak draughtsman ... Thus this book is really only an album'.[3]

This book is also a collection of what I hope are mystical snapshots inspired by a *Vorgriff* of God. Like Wittgenstein, my remarks are redundant, purposely opaque and intentionally hyperbolic - in short, all over the place. Unlike Wittgenstein, though, I have collected these fragmentary reflections into six chapters, each of which I hope exhibits a certain organic coherence. Of this, however, I am not especially sanguine.

This book is dedicated to the great Jesuit priest, scholar and teacher, Michael J. Buckley, S.J., whom I am honored to have called mentor, friend, and spiritual advisor.

1 November 2024
Feast Day of All Saints

---

[3] *Philosophical Investigations.*

Part One

God

BEYOND

CHAPTER ONE

Apophasis

God does not 'exist', but God makes possible all that exists. God is No-thing, yet all things exist in God.

'God' is a purposely non-sensical word.[4] 'God' connotes Nothing ordinary grammar can express. 'God' is the word we use to remind ourselves that whatever we apprehend of God cannot be conceptualized.

God does not 'exist' as objects in the world exist, or the world as a whole 'exists'. Yet, the world is what it is because God is who God is (Ex. 3:14).

---

[4] For Karl Rahner, the word, 'God' is intentionally non-sensical. For Rahner, 'God' is 'the final word before wordless and worshipful silence in the face of the ineffable mystery' (*Foundations of Christian Faith: An Introduction to the Idea of Christianity*, 51).

Nothing exists that is not of God, but God is not *of* the things that exist. All that exists does so because it is of God, yet God is 'completely Other' from that which God creates.

Existence is nothing apart from God. Yet, God is No-thing. Thus, creation is 'nothing from No-thing'.

Everything comes *from* God, everything is *of* God, but nothing *is* God except God Godself. The world has no existence apart from God, yet is in no manner an instantiation of God's pure Actuality.

God is the unparticipatable Mystery in which all things participate. Creation derives from God, yet no existent being is anything other than a reflection of the Divine Mystery of which it partakes.

'*What*' something is can never account for the fact '*that*' it is. Both essence ('what') and existence ('that') come from Elsewhere. The *Non-Aliud*[5] God is that 'Elsewhere'.

---

[5] '***Non Aliud***' ('Not Other') - A term made famous by Nicholas of Cusa to denote the non-competitive, totally incomprehensible 'Otherness' of God from the world, which simultaneously and paradoxically makes possible God's equally incomprehensible intimacy with all God has called into existence.

God is so completely 'Other' from everything we can know and understand, a certain kind of a-theism speaks more eloquently of God than religious rhetoric. Better a sincere atheist than a devoted believer 'who does not know what he is saying' (Lk. 9:33).

There is no need to 'gild the lily' when we apprehend God as 'Absolutely Other'. Nature itself is 'full of grace'. 'The rose without a why; she blooms because she blooms; she pays herself no attention and doesn't ask whether or not she is seen'.[6]

Knowing we are nothing apart from God, and knowing that God Himself is No-thing, we delight in the fact that we are 'nothing from Nothing'.

Everything of God is necessarily a *skandalon* (stumbling block) for human reason. So impoverished is our standard *noesis*,[7] that most of us find it outlandish that we are 'gods in God'[8] from all eternity.

---

[6] *The Mystical Poems of Angelus Silesius.*

[7] *Noesis* - the process of cognitive understanding or knowledge acquisition, particularly in the context of grasping abstract concepts or mystical truths.

[8] The 8th century Syriac spiritual writer, John of Dalyatha, summarizing the patristic tradition, says, 'You, O man, are the image of God. Do you want the image to take on the likeness of the model? . . . (then carry) wonder in your mind at his majesty, until it shines out in its glory and is changed into the likeness, until you become **'a god in God'**, having acquired the likeness of the Creator by the union which assimilates (you) to Him'. *'Letter 29. 1'* (emphasis added), cited in Norman Russell, *The Doctrine of Deification in the Greek Patristic Tradition*, 324.

God does not 'exist' as objects exist. Thus, God is non-exist*ent*, but God is not non-exist*ing*. God is *Actus Purus*[9] - the ineffable, impassible, inconceivable *Ur-sprung*[10] ('Source') of all that is.

Creation is a theophany of the character of God, and God is present to creation with an immediacy impossible for us to grasp.

As *Actus Purus*, God is what God does. God creates because of Who God *is*, not because of what God needs or wants. What God desires, God already is.

God is beyond being, yet the immanent and sustaining Source of every being. God is the inexpressible 'I AM' in which every 'it is' enjoys its existence.

God's *immanence* in the world is a function of his utter *transcendence*. It is because God is 'non-existent', that creation exists *ex nihilo*.

'Intelligibility' is something that can never be predicated of God. God is the unintelligible *Source* of intelligibility itself.

---

[9] ***Pure Act.*** According to St. Thomas Aquinas, God can be analogically described as Pure Act (*Actus Purus*), i.e., the unconditioned and ineffable Act of all acts, the Perfection of all perfections and the perfect Being of all created beings. This Pure Act is called 'being' in the strong sense or intensive *Being* (*Esse ut actus*, or *Actus essendi*) to distinguish it from *being* in the weak sense or common being (*esse commune*) of all created entities. See: *Summa Theologica*, I, Q 3, a. 4, ad. 1.

[10] ***Ur-sprung*** (German) - Source, Origin. See Philip Krill, *Ursprung: Intuitions from God-Knows- Where*.

Creation is a bold assertion of the why-less God's why-less Love. Scientific explanations account for neither the boldness nor the assertion.

God is 'beyond' the world in a way that is 'beyond' every spatial image of 'beyond'.

God is 'other' from the world in a way that is *totally* 'Other'. God is the *'other Other'*, requiring a grammar of its own that we do not possess.[11]

God does not differ from us in the way we differ from each other. God differs differently.

The Wisdom (*Sophia*) of God does not arise from the human intellect. Inspiration - the only true medium of divine revelation - arrives unconditioned, emerging serendipitously through the veil of the intellect, then making a bee-line straight to the heart.

The paradoxes in theology and philosophy are God's way of signaling 'Hands off!' to our attempts to 'unscrew the inscrutable'.

Systems are anathema to divine *Sophia* (Wisdom). Systems are for those who find the subtleties of the Spirit analytically undetectable.

---

[11] See David Burrell, *Freedom and Creation in Three Traditions* and *Creation and the God of Abraham*.

Vorgriff

Approaching God by the way of *unknowing (apophasis)*[12] is the tried and true way of apprehending God as the unseen Source and Satisfaction of all our desires.

Apophasis is ecstasy for those who enter the 'luminous darkness'. Seeking God via negation is the inner meaning of 'I sleep and my heart is awake' (Song of Songs, 5:2).

Our concepts of God are foolishness to God (1 Cor. 1:25). God is better known by the sincere atheist than by the purveyors of religious apologetics.

The *actuality (esse)* of things gives the lie to our attempts to categorize and systematize. Our greatest error is 'to confuse words with concepts and concepts with real things'.[13]

Gamaliel knew whereof he spoke (Acts 5:38-39). Better to say nothing of that which we do not understand than to say something about that which we cannot prove.

---

[12] **Apophatic theology** is a form of theological thinking which approaches God by way of negation. This method of **negative theology** arose in deference to the 'ever-greater' in God vis-a-vis anything we may predicate positively about God. *Apophasis* was an important method of the early church fathers, especially Pseudo-Dionysius the Areopagite and Maximus the Confessor. **Apophatic theology** has greatly shaped the contemplative monastic tradition of the Eastern Orthodox Churches, as well as the mystical traditions of western Christianity.

[13] J. G. Hamann, cited by Isaiah Berlin, *The Magnus of the North: J. G. Hamann and the Origins of Modern Irrationalism*, 40.

The 'existence' of God can be neither understood nor proved, since God does not exist in any manner graspable by us.

We *apprehend*[14] something of God when we acknowledge our inability to *comprehend* God. In the space of theological paralysis, we are suddenly opened to the whispers of the Spirit.

The radical uncertainty evident at the quantum level of reality is an icon of creation's *openness* to God. We are as inherently uncertain about the ultimate constituents of matter as we are of the inner workings of the Trinity.

To describe something as 'happening' is already to have acknowledged its gratuitous character. Heisenberg's uncertainty principle is as apt a description of the unpredictable epiphanies of everyday life as of subatomic particles.

God is 'Nothing', not in the sense of simple negation, but in the sense of the *insufficiency* of our affirmations. Better to abide peacefully in *apophasis* than remain restless in our questions about the 'nature' and 'attributes' of God.

---

[14] **Apprehend** means 'to grasp', 'to seize', 'to lay hold of'. In this book, *apprehend* refers to a pre-conceptual, intuitive way of 'knowing' God without any relation to our *ideas about* God. In this context, *apprehension* is to *comprehension* what contemplation is to meditation.

Our praises of God blaspheme when they pretend to objective knowledge of God. As St. Augustine says, 'the best that a human can say about God is to know how to be silent from the fullness of the wisdom of interior wealth'.[15]

Whatever we can name or describe about God is not God. The best form of God's praise is to admit we know nothing about the unknowable God. If we were to have a God whom we could know, we could not honor Him as God.

As non-objective, God has been described as Pure Act (*Actus Purus*)[16] or Pure Being. But where does this get us? Nowhere. Yet, that is exactly where we find God - No-where.

Neither God nor 'be-ing' (ex-istence) can be objectified; they can only be 'experienced', i.e., 'apprehended'. Mechanistic materialism is the result of our reification of the meta-physical.

That which we seek is seeking us.[17] When we search for God, we are like the mouse searching for the cat.[18] The *Actuality* of God (*Actus Purus*) is altogether prior to - and the sole inspiration for - our interest in God.

---

[15] As cited by Sergius Bulgakov, *Unfading Light: Contemplations and Speculations*, 144.

[16] See above, n. 9.

[17] Paraphrase of Rumi's famous quote: 'What you seek is seeking you'.

[18] So, C. S. Lewis, 'Amiable agnostics will talk cheerfully about 'man's search for God. To me, as I then was, they might as well have talked about the mouse's search for the cat'. *Surprised by Joy*, 227.

In our apprehension of God as *Actus Purus*, we glimpse the unlimited fecundity of creation, and the infinite possibilities of every eternal Now. We see, as if in a flash, that 'nothing is impossible for God' (Lk. 1:37).

Infinity plus one does not equal a number greater than infinity. Just so, God plus the world is not greater than God alone.

The world enjoys a *real* relation with God, but God admits of only a *logical* relation to the world. The asymmetry of this God-world relationship eludes any imaginable analogue.

God is an absolute Plenitude of Actuality, completely Other from the world of created, contingent entities whose existence is a participation in the unparticipatable God.

If the annihilation of matter is an illusion (e.g., $E = mc^2$), mustn't death of the spirit be even more impossible? If 'there lives the dearest freshness deep down things',[19] must not the End of all things be a theophanic Fullness beyond human imaginings?

If God is the *Archē* (Origin) and *Telos* (End) of creation, the End (*Omega*) must be in the Beginning (*Alpha*), and the Beginning must be *a function of* the End. Nothing is created that God has not already programmed for its final perfection.

---

[19] Gerard Manley Hopkins, *God's Granduer.*

Vorgriff

The present comes to us as a gift from the future, and the freshness of every present moment is a proleptic epiphany of an eschatological Newness that never ends.

Analogy is the sophianic interval between the non-existent God and the world. Here, God, the inherently Unmanifest, dis-closes Himself in that which is not-God.

'Behold, I make all things new!' (Rev. 21:5). Every present moment is a re-enactment of creation *ex nihilo* for those 'who have eyes to see' (Deut. 29:4).

There is an unbridgeable difference between the mystery of *existence* (*esse*) and the mechanics of creation (essence). In-depth understanding of quantum mechanics does not a mystic make.

Creation ex *nihilo* reveals that all things come unaccountably *from* God, are continuously dependent *upon* God, yet remain completely *other from* God. Still, it has pleased God to be irrevocably *one with* all that God creates.

Since God is the beginning and end of all things, protology and eschatology are a single mystery in God. This means that creation is complete only in its glorious consummation in God.

Love must be the deepest dimension of every being, since all that exists comes from God who is Love (1 Jn. 4:16). Creation is 'love from Love' - an extension and expression of God in that which is *other* from God.

Nothing that exists or is allowed to exist is not of God. Everything begins as an expression of God's goodness, and nothing ends without having perfectly accomplished the divine purpose for which it was created (Isa. 55:11).

There is a mystical 'communication of idioms' (*communicatio idiomatum*) within the Trinity that pre-exists that of the Incarnation, namely that *'God is what God does, and God does what God is'*. This is the theological and metaphysical basis for insisting we are 'gods in God'.

We enjoy a *participative* union *with* God,[20] as well as a limited autonomy *in* God. In God's radical *Otherness*, we are, as it were, 'on our own', and in God's ubiquitous *Presence*, we are, as it were, one *with* God.

Our absolute *otherness from* God is identical with our inseparable *union with* God. Ontic alienation from God is impossible, given God's prevenient inclusion of us in his uncreated Love (cf. Jer. 1:5; Eph. 1:4).

---

[20] See Andrew Davison, *Participation in God: A Study in Christian Doctrine and Metaphysics*.

Because our existence is, in every way, *derivative of* God, we are nothing in ourselves but everything in God. As eternally-chosen expressions of the God who is Love (1 Jn. 4:16), we are instantiations of Divine Love in finite form.

At every moment, our lives are creative expressions of God's self-glorification. At every instant, we are 'Yes'd!' into existence by the One who is pleased to glorify Himself in us, and us in Him (Jn. 17:10).

We *are* before we are *this* or *that*. Bliss arises when we recognize ourselves as ontologically prior to any definition we give of ourselves.

We know ourselves to be 'of God' *through* God. It is God Himself who awakens us to our derivative, yet ontologically real, 'participation' in God's own Life.

Creation is '*of God*', both as an expression of God's unconditioned Goodness, and as a 'sacrament' of God's abiding Presence within creation.

The 'splendor' of creation (think: 'beautiful sunset', 'majestic mountains') is the shimmering of God's glory in condensed form. Beauty is a theophany of God's Love, accommodated to the limits of human vision.

Our desire for God is the Presence of God manifest within the limits of human finitude. God is a Mystery of Pure Desire, desiring that we love Him as he loves us.

The reification of God is theological suicide. The objectification of be-ing - 'to be' - is metaphysical masochism.

'Existence' itself is an expression of God's uncontainable desire to share Godself with all that is not-God.

CHAPTER TWO

Ur-Kenosis

God pours Himself out without diminishment. Better put: God's own self-actualization consists in a kind of divine *Ur-kenosis*[21] in which the Father 'empties' Himself (without loss) in the begetting of his Son, and together, they 'breathe forth' the Holy Spirit as the Life of their inner Life.

Self-transcendence and self-dis-possession are synonymous in God. God is a Mystery of tri-personal self-expropriation that is also God's self-actualization.

---

[21] ***Ur-kenosis*** – In German, the prefix *ur* indicates an original or earliest form of something. *Ur-kenosis*, then, means the original or first instance of 'self-emptying'. Hans Urs von Balthasar (*Theo-Dramatics, IV,* 331) speaks of three 'cascading *kenoses*', flowing, as it were, from the Original or *Ur-kenosis* beginning with the Father in the Trinity: '[A] first *kenosis* of the Father, expropriating Himself by generating' the consubstantial Son. Almost automatically, this first *kenosis* expands to a *kenosis* involving the whole Trinity. For the Son could not be consubstantial with the Father except by self-expropriation; and their We, that is, the Spirit, must also be God if he is to be the 'personal seal of that self-expropriation that is identical in Father and Son ... This primal *kenosis* makes possible all other kenotic movements of God into the world; they are simply its consequence'.

'Letting-go' is a participation in the *Ur-kenosis* of God. We partake of God's self-surrender (*Ur-kenosis*) in every action of joyous relinquishment (*Gelassenheit*).[22]

Diminishment and death are beautiful images of the trinitarian *Ur-kenosis*. Our deification is made perfect when we consent to passing away joyfully in imitation of God's own self-surrender.

God is a triune Mystery of self-emptying Love. The Father 'empties Himself' in the begetting of his Son, and the Son 'empties Himself' in obedience to the Father. The Spirit is the *Dynamis* of this Mystery of self-dispossession.

Death is identical with Life in the heart of the Trinity: the Father 'dies to Himself' in the begetting of his Son, and the Son 'dies to Himself' in doing as the Father commands (Jn. 5:19). The Spirit makes possible this Life-in-death.

Brahman surrenders Itself to *Atman*, and *Atman* fulfills itself in surrendering to *Brahman*.[23] Both 'surrenders' result, not in self-annihilation, but in self-actualization.

---

[22] *Gelassenheit* - a German word for 'tranquil submission', 'letting go', or 'divine releasement'. It is widespread in the Christian mystical tradition, especially as found in the writing of Meister Eckhart. See Philip Krill, *Gelassenheit: Day-by-Day with Meister Eckhart*.

[23] *Brahman* - Sanskrit synonym for 'God', i.e., the ultimate, all-encompassing reality that is eternal, unchanging, and beyond human perception. *Atman* - Sanskrit term for the innermost self or soul, often mistaken as separate from Brahman due to ignorance.

God is an *Ur-kenotic* Mystery of divine deference. God 'backs off' from interfering in human affairs so that, in God's apparent absence, we may learn to discern and practice God's unassuming, deferential Presence.

Who God is is ever-greater, and eternally prior to, *what* God is. *Personhood* precedes and sublates 'being' in God.[24] There is no 'nature' of God other than the Mystery of God's trinitarian Personhood.

Unity differentiates, and perfect unity differentiates perfectly.[25] Herein lies the perennial conundrum of 'the One and the many' that finds its source and solution in the Trinity.

The mystery of *'Das Ganze-im-Fragment'*[26] ('One and the many', 'Whole and the part') finds its 'resolution' within the Trinity. Here, metaphysics is both relativized and legitimated as a necessary but insufficient resource on the Mind's Road to God.[27]

If we apprehend the *Ur-kenosis* of God, we aspire to a similar 'self-emptying'. We desire the dissolution of everything about ourselves other than our 'I-am-ness', which is our participation in God as the primordial 'I AM' (Ex. 3:17).

---

[24] For a detailed exposition of this counter-intuitive perspective, see John D. Zizoulas, *Being as Communion* and *Communion and Otherness*.

[25] Phrase attributed, without specific reference in his writings, to Pierre Teilhard de Chardin. See: https://quoteinvestigator.com/2019/06/20/spiritual.

[26] See Hans Urs von Balthasar, *Man in History: A Theological Anthropology* (Original title: *Das Ganze im Fragment*).

[27] St. Bonaventure, *The Mind's Road to God*.

Christian vision is altogether eschatological. Participating in trinitarian self-transcendence (*Ur-kenosis*), we experience every moment filled with the Light of God's future kingdom (Rev. 21:23).

Christ is the Incarnation of the Father's self-donation, and the instrument of the Spirit's self-dispersion. Christ is the sacrament of the self-dispossessing God (Acts 17:23).

Jesus, 'wearied and tired' from his journey on earth (Jn. 4:6), is identical with God's Eternal Word. The weakness and limitations of human flesh are the perfect revelation of Christ's *kenosis* in the heart of the Trinity.

Christ's apprehension of God as 'greater than I' (Jn. 14:28) is so complete that he can also say, 'the Father and I are one' (Jn. 10:30). In Christ, we are both 'one with' and 'other than' the ineffable Mystery known as 'God'.

Nothing is accurate about Christ that is not somewhat cryptic. Christ is a scandal (*skandalon*) to normal human thinking. In the *skandalon* of Christ, we are given a *Vorgriff* of Christ's - and our - transcendental oneness with God.

Presence[28] is supreme availability. It was Christ's eternal *availability* to the Father that made it possible for Him to become the Incarnation of God's Presence to the world.

---

[28] See below, chapter 5.

Humanity was eternally conceived by God with an eye to the Incarnation. Humanity and divinity are perfectly matched in the Eternal Word, even 'before the foundation of the world' (Eph. 1:4).

Our capacity for 'rising above ourselves' is a participation in the 'Ascension' of Christ. As the Eternal *Logos*, Christ is 'lifted up' in order to 'draw all things to Himself' (Jn. 12:32).[29]

Absent epiphanic illumination, religion does not inspire. Religion is ossified inspiration, but inspiration makes religion theophanic.

How can clerics bear to hear themselves preach if they do not experience themselves like Moses before the burning bush (Ex. 3:2), or like the bedazzled apostles atop Mt. Tabor (Mk. 9:6)?

Christ calls Himself 'the Resurrection and the Life' because, 'being present' to his Father, (Lk. 5:16), he experiences an eternal 'lifting up' that is a gracious manifestation of the 'God of the living, not of the dead' (Lk. 20:38).

Christ experienced Himself as the *Ur-sakrament*[30] of the impassible yet self-dispossessing God. Drawn to Christ, as if by a spiritual magnet, we become partakers of his eternal union with the Father.

---

[29] David Bentley Hart (*The New Testament: A Translation*) translates this phrase, '*drag everyone to me*'.

[30] *Ur-sakrament* - A phrase popularized by Karl Rahner to refer to Jesus Christ as the primordial sacrament of God's desire to give Himself completely to the whole of humanity.

The Incarnation is affirmation that finitude (limitedness) is not a *fall* from grace. In Christ, the finite and the Infinite enjoy a non-competitive, if asymmetrical, co-inherence.[31] The 'minimum' and the 'maximum' are indistinguishable in God.[32]

Both our existence and our essence are sharing in the plenitude of the Mystery of God. The created and the uncreated both happen within God, and both are present in us, albeit in a different way.

Nature and supernature are not two distinct levels of reality, just as God and creation are not two incompatible objects set over against one another in unbridgeable antithesis. Otherwise, our *Vorgriff* of God would be impossible.

God's desire is that we desire God to satisfy our desires. Thus, when Christ says to the Woman at the Well (Jn. 4), 'I thirst', his meaning is clear: 'My thirst is to satisfy your thirst with the Living Water that I am'.

Why did God create a world inevitably embroiled in countless contradictions? Answer: So the divine mercy of Christ, His Son, would be made manifest in time and space.[33]

---

[31] On the notion of 'non-competitive co-inherence', see Robert Barron, *The Priority of Christ: Towards a Postliberal Catholicism*.

[32] Nicolas of Cusa, *On Learned Ignorance*.

[33] So, St. Irenaeus: 'Since he who saves already existed, it was necessary that he who would be saved should come into existence, that the One who saves should not exist in vain'. *Against Heresies*, 3.22.3, quoted in John Behr, *The Mystery of Christ: Life in Death*, 77.

Christ is God's pre-eternal *Alpha* in whom the world's *coincidentia oppositorum* are conceived. Christ is God's eschatological *Omega* in whom all polarities, polemics and problems of the world are reconciled.

Christ's self-presence as 'begotten of God' enables Him to love his killers. Likewise, it is our awareness that we are 'gods in God'[34] that makes it possible for us to 'forgive our enemies and do good to those who hate us' (Lk. 6:27-28).

The mercy of Christ is a source of mendacity for the world. Christ's admonition, 'Learn the meaning, 'I desire mercy not sacrifice' (Mt. 9:13; cf. Hos. 6:6) is an uncomfortable command for those promoting a sacrificial mentality.

Knowing Himself to be God's 'stumbling block' (*skandalon*) for many of those he encountered (Mt. 11:6; 1 Cor. 1:123), Jesus nevertheless dies of joy (Heb. 2:15) because of his fidelity to the Father. We are saved, not by faith *in* Christ, but through 'the faithfulness *of* Jesus Christ' (*pistis Christou*).[35]

---

[34] See above, n. 8.

[35] ***Pistis Christou*** ('The faithfulness of Jesus Christ') - The ultimate meaning of 'salvation' is 'participation in' the ***pistis Christou,*** i.e., in 'the faithfulness of Jesus Christ'. For an extended discussion on salvation as participation in the 'faithfulness of Christ' (***pistis Christou***), see N. T. Wright, *Pauline Perspectives: Essays on Paul,* 529-533.

Christ's admonition to unlimited forgiveness was, for the political and religious authorities, the unforgivable sin. No ideology can long survive without an enemy against which it defines itself.

Christ's message of 'enemy love' made of Him the #1 enemy of both church and state. Caiaphas and Pilate 'became friends that day' (Lk. 23:12) because, for them, 'the enemy of my enemy is my friend'.

Christ plunges his listeners into personal and religious miasma so that their misery might be turned to mercy. Christ offends only to awaken.

Evil is permitted by God as 'the absence of good' so the Incarnation of Goodness (Christ) might reveal the 'principalities and powers' of malevolence as instruments (and recipients) of Divine Mercy.

A hyperbolic aesthetic is the only grammar appropriate to the non-existent God and his Incarnate Word. The gospel is not the gospel if not experienced as preposterous.

If the gospel does not render us incredulous, it has not been heard. The *kerygma* of Christ is outlandish, both in what it promises and what it demands; yet, what it demands is made possible only by what it promises.

It is the ability of Christ to leave his listeners *incredulous* that makes his *evangel* (gospel) such a scandal (*skandalon*).

The *skandalon* created by Christ bespeaks an intimacy with God unknown to his interlocutors. Experiencing Himself as filled with the Divine Presence, Christ speaks for God *as* God.

It is from the 'impassible God' that the Incarnation comes forth as the theandric[36] expression of God's infinitely passionate Love.

The Incarnation is the finest expression of God's transcendence. It is precisely because God is so 'totally Other' from us that he could, and did, become one of us.

The world is created to be - and to become - the vessel and sacrament of Absolute Being. The cosmos called into existence to be 'God-ified' in Christ.

The divine humanity of the Eternal Word (Christ) is the Divine Seed implanted by the Father in the soil of the world to be the leaven for its final transfiguration.

The creation of the world and the Incarnation ultimately elide. 'Always, and in all things, the *Logos*, who is God, desires to realize the mystery of His embodiment'.[37]

---

[36] *Theandric* - a term denoting the characteristic activity of the God-man, Jesus the Christ, in which the acts or operations, both his divine and human natures, cooperate.

[37] St. Maximus the Confessor, *Ambigua ad Johannem*, 7.

23

Vorgriff

The Paraclete 'teaches us all things' (Jn. 14:26), even about 'the deep things of God (1 Cor. 2:10). Failing a *Vorgriff* of the Spirit's inner anointing, Scripture remains a 'dead letter' (Rom. 7:6) and religion, the routine of 'dead men walking'.

Neither creation nor the Incarnation are complete until all things are reconciled in Christ. Christ will 'fill all things' (Col. 1:23) after he 'draws all things to Himself' (Jn. 12:32) in a mutually-constitutive *Plērōma*[38] of created and Uncreated Beauty.

Through his open side on the Cross, and with his final breath, Christ bequeathed to the world the same Spirit by which he was born of the Virgin. The Spirit of Christ is active in the world until such time as God will 'be all in all' (1 Cor. 15:28).

The 'Whole Christ'[39] includes all things - lifted up, drawn to, and completely transfigured in Christ as the ascended Lord (Jn. 12:32; Col. 1:20). The 'Total Christ' (*Totus Christus*)[40] is the Incarnate Word 'come to full stature' (Eph. 4:13).

---

[38] *Plērōma* – Greek word translated 'fullness', or 'totality'. In Scripture (cf. Jn. 1:12-14; Eph. 1:22-23; Col. 1:19; 2:9-10), it refers to the fullness of God in Christ and the recapitulation and redemption of all things in Christ.

[39] See Emile Mersch, *The Whole Christ: The Historical Development of the Doctrine of the the Mystical Body in Scripture and Tradition.*

[40] 'Christ and his Church thus together make up the 'whole Christ' (*Christus Totus*). The Church is one with Christ'. *Catechism of the Catholic Church*, 795.

Christ disarms evil, not by opposition, but by absorption. Christ makes of Himself the world's whipping boy, so that his bruised, beaten and bloody body might serve as the mirror in which, horrified by their own actions, purveyors of violence might turn 'their swords into plowshares' (Isa. 2:4; cf. Mk. 15:39).

Christ overcomes evil by becoming its innocent victim. Christ defeats evil by becoming the willing target of murderous lies and gross deceptions. Christ unmasks evil by revealing, at the cost of his own life, its inveterate ugliness.

Until we can see the beauty of the crucified Christ, we have understood nothing of the ways of God. *Dereliction without despair* is the glory of the divine Scapegoat.

Christ's Agony in the garden was his awareness of the unselfconsciousness of 'the crowd' (Mk. 9:19).[41] Christ fled from situations where those 'crowding in on Him' lacked situational-awareness (Mk. 4:36).

The *Logos* of God subverts the world's logic of retributive vengeance. Christ's Cross is the stick thrown into the gears of geo-political power, grinding them to a halt.

---

[41] For Jesus' aversion to 'the crowd' as the occasion of sin, see Robert Hamerton-Kelly, *The Gospel and the Sacred: Poetics of Violence in Mark.*

What we do to anyone, we do to God (cf. Mt. 25:46). This is because, since from all eternity, the whole of humanity is included in God's Divine Word.

Christ's *silence* before his accusers speaks more eloquently than all the world's wisdom.

Christ reveals the trinitarian communion of divine Love as the saving alternative to the political and religious matrices of deception.

Christ is a 'stumbling block' to most, and a 'stepping stone' to some. In either case, there is no getting around Christ without undergoing a crisis.

Christ came to bring, 'not peace but division' (Jn. 14:27; Lk. 12:51). But even for those who stumble and fall, Christ is the Good Samaritan who picks them up, cares for them, and carries them back to his Father's house (Lk. 10:33-35).

It is the *crucified* Christ whose *ignominy* reveals the world's structural mercilessness. It is the *risen* Christ who discloses a glorious End to the world's agonizing suicide.

Christ's Agony in the garden (Lk. 22:44), and his tears over Jerusalem (Lk. 19:41), bespeak divine *grief*, not divine wrath. Christ embraced a horrific death to unmask the world's death-wish.

Christ's anger at the charlatans who 'cleanse the outside of the cup' but leave the inside 'filled with rapaciousness' (Lk. 11:39) are expressions of divine *exasperation*. It is our *ignorance* of the evil, embedded in our ordinary actions, that is the occasion for Christ's Divine Pity.[42]

Christ explodes transactional paradigms for right relation with God, replacing them with a unifying vision of transfiguration. Surrender, not stoic sacrifice, is the *sine quo non* for our transformation in Christ.

Christ's Passion is his realization that his life has been an exquisite failure. Jesus' Agony is his awareness he has become 'a near occasion of sin' for those who, in their recoil from his gospel of love, plan for his demise.

Christ scandalizes our religious sensibilities so that, in our belligerence and bewilderment, we might 'come to our senses' and return to 'our Father's house' (Lk. 15:1-24).

Those existentially in touch with the *Vorgriff* that constitutes their natural orientation towards God share in the Agony of Christ. Experiencing the world as shot through with Divine Presence, they agonize over the world's ignorance of 'what makes for peace' (Rom. 14:19).

---

[42] Gerald Vann, O.P., *The Divine Pity: A Study in the Social Implications of the Beatitudes.*

Didache (dogmatic teaching) has replaced *kerygma* (inspiring proclamation) as the fiat currency of contemporary Christianity, which is the real reason institutional churches are going bankrupt.

The gospel of the crucified Christ will always be a stumbling block (*skandalon*) for those who attempt to systematize or institutionalize it.

'He came to his own and his own received Him not' (Jn. 1:11). In 2,000 years, nothing much has changed.

Christ is the undigestible 'bread of life' (Jn. 6:48) in the belly of the beast. Christ makes the world sick to its stomach so that, in its distress, it may 'come to its senses' (Lk. 15:17).

God never 'punishes' except to 'purify'. Christ never rebukes except to redeem. The Spirit never upbraids, save to uplift.

There is no 'wrath of God' other than that which seeks to awaken a somnambulant world to a wondrous Love beyond its wildest dreams.

Our love for God is also God's love for us. 'In this is love, not that we loved God but that God has loved us'(1 Jn. 4:10).

Our love for God and God's love for us is of a piece with the Son's love of the Father, and the Father's love of the Son. Nothing we do for God has God not already done for us in Christ 'before the foundation of the world' (Eph. 1:4).

The Incarnation is the supreme expression of God's aseity.[43] The higher God is beyond the reach of our intelligence, the more intimately God manifests his Presence in the woof and warp of our existence.

At the heart of reality is the theophanic power of God's creative Seed. Christ is the divine 'Seed' of the Father, planted in the soil of the world, 'for the life of the world' (Jn. 6:33).

A final flourishing of the cosmos in an *Apokatastasis*[44] and *Plērōma*[45] of unimaginable glory is the purpose the world was created in the first place.

We come from glory and are destined for glory.[46] Whatever appears to go right or wrong in the process is ultimately destined to 'work for good' (Rom. 8:28; Phil. 2:13).

---

[43] *Aseity* - a term indicating God's independent 'otherness' and transcendence from created, finite being. God is, so to speak, *the unconditioned condition for the possibility of existence*. The *aseity* of God means that He is the One in whom all other things find their source, existence, and continuance.

[44] *Apokatastasis* - Greek term referring to 'restoration'. The 'restoration of all things' is prevalent among certain Patristic Era theologians regarding God's universally salvific, eschatological intentions for all creation, including that which was 'lost' through the Fall.

[45] See above, n. 38.

[46] See Alvin Kimel, *Destined for Joy: The Gospel of Universal Salvation*.

The redemptive love of God in Christ is as irrepressible as it is irresistible. Notions of human responsibility pale in light of God's pre-eternal desire that 'all persons be saved and come to a knowledge of the truth' (2 Tim. 1:4).

To believe human sin could prove more invincible than the desire of God 'that all be saved' (2 Tim. 1:4) is to make Satan the co-equal of God. It is satanic to believe that Satan could eternally outsmart God in his handling of human beings.

We are called to rest contentedly in our *ignorance* of God and other people's business. Every such act of self-surrender unites us more completely with God than all the analysis in the world.

For Christ, the distinction between nature and grace does not exist. Christ stands atop Mt. Tabor, transfigured as the pinnacle of a world that is, by nature, 'full of grace'.

'Behold, I make all things new!' (Rev. 21:5). If we took these words seriously, we would acquire the intellectual *caution* of Nicodemus (Jn. 7:50-51) and the religious *humility* of Gamaliel (Acts 5:38-39).

Christ apprehends the transcendent God as exquisitely present to every particle of creation. Christ lives nowhere other than in the heart of the world and in the epicenter of God's Eternal Now.

God includes the whole of humanity in the humanity of his pre-existent Son (Jn. 1:1). We are creations and extensions of God's own divine-humanity for the divinization of the world.

God, it is true, 'became man' in Jesus, yet, strictly speaking, God cannot 'become' anything God wasn't already from eternity. In Christ, we have always been, and will be forever, 'gods in God'[47].

It is a function of God's absolute transcendence that humanity inhabits a place in God. Only a God who is 'completely Other' can 'become man' such that man, in Christ, can become God.[48]

Because the whole of humanity was 'made sacred' in Christ from all eternity, everything divine is also human. Nothing can 'become' anything that was not already something divine in God.

God says of his creation, 'It is very good', because every phenomenon is an icon and efficacious pledge of the unspeakable Goodness and Love making it possible. *That Which* (God) makes phenomena possible is infinitely more beautiful than phenomena themselves.

---

[47] See above, n. 8.

[48] 'God became man so man could become God' (St. Athanasius, *On the Incarnation*, 54).

Christ, in his Incarnation, reveals Himself to be the *Logos* of God, i.e., the visible manifestation of the inner 'structure' ('Mind' and 'Heart') of God as Love (1 Jn. 4:16).[49] Every essence in nature (*logoi*) is a sacramental expression of God's *Logos*.[50]

The *logoi* of creation must necessarily be instantiations of the *Logos* of God because 'Every effect remains in its cause, proceeds from it, and reverts upon it'.[51] God is the uncaused Cause that causes all other causes.

Matter is frozen light, and light is liquid love. The whole of creation is a 'flowing forth' from a trinitarian Wellspring of eternally circulating Love.

'He came to his own and his own received Him not, but to everyone who did receive Him, he gave the power to become children of God (Jn. 1:11-12). Those who have no religion are often more receptive to the revelation of Christ than the religiously righteous who believe they have 'no need' of such a revelation' (Lk. 15:7).

---

[49] See Benedict XVI, *Dogma and Preaching: Applying Christian Doctrine to Daily Life*, 93-95.

[50] ***Logoi*** – term used by Greek-speaking theologians to indicate the inner principle, essence, or intentionality behind all things, which in turn explains their natural participation or fellowship with the **Logos**, who in Scripture is identified as none other than the Son of God Himself, the Father's agent of creation. The relation of ***logoi*** to **Logos** is mystically described by St. Maximus the Confessor. See Lars Thunberg, *Microcosm and Mediator: The Theological Anthropology of Maximus the Confessor.*

[51] Proclus, *The Elements of Theology*, proposition 35, cited in Eric D. Perl, *Theophany: The Neoplatonic Philosophy of Dionysius the Areopagite*, 35.

Scripture, like all instruments of religion, is relatively worthless if not approached analogically and anagogically. Only when approached with an intuitive apprehension of the Trinity, and a vision of a final Fullness of all things (*Plērōma*) in Christ as *Totus Christus*, do the words of Scripture communicate the transcendent Wisdom of God.

God's love is a why-less love,[52] but it is not without its *Logos* (logic). The fact that God *is* love' (1 Jn. 4:8), is the 'reason' (*logos*) God loves without a reason.

God is as Jesus does. Jesus, like his Father, does what he does *because of who he is*, not for any other 'reason'.

The world is a safety net that Jesus had no interest in using. Christ's high-wire act is one we cannot imitate without falling flat on our faces. The only alternative is to find our balance point *within* Christ, not alongside of Him.[53]

The deification of humanity and the transfiguration of the cosmos is the purpose of creation. 'All things were made for Him, all things made through Him; He is before all else that is, and in Him all things find existence and coherence (Col. 1:16-17; Jn. 1:3).

---

[52] A phrase common in the writings of Meister Eckhart. See: Paul E. Szarmach, *An Introduction to the Medieval Mystics of Europe*, 253.

[53] St. Paul uses the phrase 'in Christ' (*en Christo*) over 165 times in his writings to convey our 'participative union' with Christ. See the brilliant summary of Pauline mysticism, particularly regarding St. Paul's 'doctrine of participation', in James D. G. Dunn, *The Theology of Paul the Apostle*, 390-410.

Existence itself bears the watermark of Christ. Finitude, most especially death, is a reflection of, and participation in, the divine *kenosis* of Christ who 'did not deem equality with God something to be grasped at' (Phil. 2:6), but who pours Himself out within both the immanent and economic Trinity.[54]

The demise of institutional Christianity is the fulfillment of the gospel. 'Christianity is the only religion that has foreseen its own failure'.[55] This inverse logic is better understood by the church's adversaries than by its advocates.

'Surrender is victory' in the kingdom of God. 'Less is more' is the calculus of Christ. 'Killing with kindness' is the only command issued by the Lamb who is slain (Rev. 5:12).

Christ's *kenosis* is our *theosis*, and our *theosis* is a participation in God's *Ur-kenosis*.

When we experience the world as the creative extension of the inner-trinitarian *Ur-kenosis*, we regard everyone and everything as sacred, and nothing and no one as our possession. Our only desire is to be an instrument of God's own Divine Releasement (*Gelassenheit*).

---

[54] The *immanent Trinity* is the inner life of Godself - a Mystery inaccessible to human comprehension. The *economic Trinity* is the manifestation of Godself in what God has created. For an explication of Karl Rahner's Rule ('The economic Trinity is the immanent Trinity)', see Fred R. Sanders, *The Image of the Immanent Trinity: Rahner's Rule and the Theological Interpretation of Scripture.*

[55] René Girard, cited in Cynthia L. Haven, *All Desire is a Desire for Being.*

'Detachment' is too rigid a word, 'surrender' too defeatist a term, and 'acceptance' too stoic a way to describe the exquisite, interior 'releasement' that characterizes those who truly 'know' God. Theirs is a joy-filled 'letting go' (*Gelassenheit*) which they experience as a participation in the *Ur-kenosis* of the Trinity.

God's *Ur-kenosis* is the Source and template for humility. Our self-transcendence, like that of God's, is fulfilled in self-emptying.

The image in the mirror is entirely derivative of, and has nothing in comparison with, the One whose countenance it mirrors. Apprehending our glorious identity as 'images of God' in our self-transcendence leads to humility, not to pride.

We can never transcend the 'self' that is capable of self-transcendence. Our likeness to God - who is an *Ur-kenosis* of self-transcendence - will always mirror the One whose Face we reflect.

God makes his Presence known in the first movement of our openness to that which is 'other' from ourselves. Every act of receptivity is a participation in a certain 'openness' and self-surrender (*Ur-kenosis*) in God from which creation emerges *ex nihilo*.

CHAPTER THREE

Vorgriff

What God has 'hidden from the clever and the theologically wise' (Mt. 11:25; 1 Cor. 1:19), he has revealed to those, like Mary, who know, 'Nothing is impossible with God'. (Lk. 1:37).

We apprehend God everywhere or we apprehend God nowhere. Yet, even when we apprehend God everywhere, we also apprehend God *as* Nowhere.

Anyone who knows God as *Actus Purus* remains speechless before the mystery of existence. Only those possessed of an existential 'intuition of being'[56] apprehend the 'Presence' of God.

---

[56] *Intuition of Being* - a phrase popularized by French philosopher Jacques Maritain, amplifying a similar, metaphysical insight of St. Thomas Aquinas. According to Maritain, this intuition of being 'is a perception direct and immediate …. a very simple sight, superior to any discursive reasoning or demonstration [… of] a reality which it touches and which takes hold of it' (*Preface to Metaphysics*, 50–51). For a fuller explanation, see: William Sweet, '*Jacques Maritain*' (*Stanford Encyclopedia of Philosophy*).

Vorgriff

To deny the 'existence' of God is to make room for the 'experience' of God.[57] The encounter with God is, at its most immediate level, a mystic event involving three dimensions: Being (*Sat*) Consciousness (*Chit*) and Bliss (*Ananda*).[58]

Reification (objectification) is the death of metaphysics, which begins and ends with an 'intuition of being', and a *Vorgriff* of God as *Actus Purus* (Pure Act).

It is impossible to perceive any object without simultaneously apprehending, albeit inchoately, the infinite Horizon of Being which makes the perception possible. God is only ever apprehended as the ineffable, unthematic Ground of Intelligibility itself.

God is not an object, and God can never be objectively known. 'God' is, by definition, inconceivable. Yet, as the ever-revealing, ever-receding 'Principle' of all human knowledge and reality, God is always more self-evident than evidence itself.

Our 'awareness' (*Vorgriff*) of God remains forever opaque. Even in the beatific vision, God remains as ungraspable as our desire for God remains insatiable.

---

[57] David Bentley Hart, *The Experience of God: Being, Consciousness, Bliss.*
[58] *Sacchidānanda* is a Hindu term that connotes the divine Bliss (*Ananda*) that arises within us when our Awareness (*Chit*) rests in Being (*Sat*), not in thinking.

Creation is altogether *of* God, even as God is altogether *not* of creation. Recognizing our inability to conceive of God is the only hermeneutical posture in which we catch a glimpse of God's immanence.

God is tacitly apprehended (*Vorgriff*) in *every* act of thinking and willing. God is present as both the indictment and enticement of our unrestricted desires to know and to have.

Our *Vorgriff* of God is also the revelation of our inclusion in the Life of God. We cannot 'know' God, even via *Vorgriff*, without knowing ourselves to be one with God.

There is an unbridgeable gap between our *Vorgriff* of God and our conceptual knowledge of God. Our conceptual mind cannot contain *That Which* it ineluctably seeks.

Our *Vorgriff* of God is a trans-cognitive apprehension of *That Which* we cannot know. The strangeness of this way of putting things is of a piece with God's revelation that his Name remains forever unpronounceable (Ex. 6:3).

Vorgriff

A disposition of 'letting go' (*Gelassenheit, Abgeschiedenheit*)[59] accrues naturally in our *Vorgriff* of God. When we apprehend God as non-conceptually present to everything and everyone, there is no need to strive after anything.

Abiding in our *Vorgriff* of God, we can 'abandon all particular forms of devotion, our only prayer practice being simple attention'.[60] Through unfiltered *openness* to all that is, we apprehend God as the Backlight of our attention.

Our *Vorgriff* of God includes the ancillary apprehension of ourselves as beloved creatures swimming in a Boundless Ocean of love. We are *in* God as fish are in the water; but, unlike fish, our *Vorgriff* of God makes us conscious of the ineffable Presence giving us life.

Our *Vorgriff* of God is commensurate with our inherent nescience. We are as intrinsically incapable of conceptualizing God as we are of being completely culpable in our actions. Our inveterate ignorance is both an epistemological and ethical grace from God.

God is Pure Actuality (*Actus Purus*). God is the Inside of the inside of things. God is what makes the *ad infinitum* of human transcendence possible.

---

[59] Synonyms used by Meister Eckhart to indicate the 'divine releasement' characteristic of the Godhead. See Reiner Schürmann, *Wandering Joy: Meister Eckhart, Mystic and Philosopher.*

[60] *Practice of the Presence of God*, 6th Letter.

To grasp the inscape[61] of things is to catch a glimpse of the ungraspable God. To see that 'the rose is without 'why', that it blooms because it blooms',[62] and that it smells as it smells, is to catch a whiff of God's incomparable fragrance.

In every act of thinking and desiring, God entices us towards Absolute goodness, beauty and truth (i.e., God Himself). In so doing, God also indicts our identification of the Absolute with any good, beauty or truth other than Godself.

The infinite Horizon present in every human act can be neither described nor grasped by anything other than a *relinquishment* of our desire to describe or grasp it.

The 'conditions making for the possibility' of anything are themselves not things. God is the unconditional Condition for the possibility of all conditions of possibility.

---

[61] *Inscape* is an enigmatic concept about individuality and uniqueness derived by the poet Gerard Manley Hopkins from the ideas of the medieval philosopher John Duns Scotus. Hopkins uses the term *'Inscape'* to connote the distinctive design that constitutes individual identity. Each being in the universe 'selves', that is, enacts its identity. As the most highly 'selved' being in the universe, the human person is able to recognize the inscape of other existent things. Ultimately, this apprehension of inscape of anything leads us to Christ, for the individual identity of any object is the stamp of Christ, the divine *Logos*, upon and within it.

[62] A famous quote by Angelus Silesius (1624–1677). He was a German mystic, known as the *Prophet of the Ineffable*. He was also a poet, priest and physician.

The existence of anything simultaneously constellates, in an unthematic way, the conditions for its own manifestation. *That which is manifest never is so without the co-presence of the un-manifest Horizon of its own intelligibility.*

Every foreground presumes a Background which can never be averted to directly without constellating an even deeper, wider and equally opaque Background. The Unmanifest can never be fully manifest, yet the latter never exists without the former.

God is to the world as negative space is to great works of art.[63] God is able to be 'seen' only as the baffling Nothingness from within which creation stands forth *ex nihilo*.

The limits of our conceptual knowledge are an invitation from God to prefer divine *Sophia* to human speculations. We are deified with God's sophianic Spirit when we abandon analysis and abide in the luminous darkness of our *Vorgriff* of God.

When we seek to make explicit our *tacit* apprehension of God (*Vorgriff*), God 'recedes', as it were, from view. God is experienced only ever 'negatively', i.e., as the indefinable End of our unrestricted desires to know and to have.

---

[63] For stunning examples of the power of negative space, see: Creative Bloq Staff. *'Negative Space: 24 Brilliant Examples'*. Creative Bloq, 20 May 2019.

Our experience is necessarily self-transcendent, but our self-transcendence is not necessarily experienced as such. A *Vorgriff* of God's Presence, and of our participation in God, is as elusive as a dog trying to catch its tail.

We know ourselves as the knower in every act of knowing, though this self-awareness is more tacit than explicit. Yet, even in an act of intentional awareness of our self-awareness, a deeper, unthematic self-awareness and self-presencing remains. It is in this inexhaustible wellspring of self-knowledge that a *Vorgriff* of God also abides.

Our *Vorgriff* of God as the Infinite Condition for the possibility of our existence is metaphysical affirmation that 'we are not human beings having a spiritual experience, but spiritual beings having a human experience'.[64]

The transcendental 'Background' presumed by our unrestricted desire to know can only ever be experienced. It cannot be 'demonstrated', save as an 'apprehension' (*Vorgriff*) of an Infinite Intelligibility making possible our infinite desire to know.

The most intellectually and spiritually mature disposition is 'to become as a little child' (Mt. 18:4). Children know, by way of intuition (*Vorgriff*), what so-called sophisticated adults have forgotten, i.e., the inexplicably-gracious *givenness* of the world.

---

[64] Phrase attributed, without specific reference in his writings, to Pierre Teilhard de Chardin. See: '*You Are Not a Human Being Having a Spiritual Experience. You Are a Spiritual Being Having a Human Experience*' – Quote Investigator®. 20 June 2019.

Vorgriff

All scientific and spiritual enlightenment derives from keeping alive a child-like apprehension of the intrinsic luminosity of a cosmos that need not be.

A *Vorgriff* of God arises when we 'back off' and 'make way' for anything or anyone. God is fleetingly apprehended in the *relief* we feel every time we 'loosen our grip' on life, 'letting things unfold organically'.

The negative space in art can never be made a focal point of our attention without destroying the artwork's inherent beauty.[65] Similarly, we cannot conceptually advert to God without God 'disappearing' from view.

Two kinds of awareness are present in every rational act - focal and tacit.[66] That *of which* we are *tacitly* aware can never be made an object of *focal* attention without bringing into tacit awareness another set of implicit conditions for the possibility of what was just made explicit. There is no end to how far this re-framing can continue.

Only a *Vorgriff* of our lives as 'hidden with Christ in God's (Col. 3:3) provides a proleptic glimpse of our eternal, divinely-human identity in God. We are 'hidden' in God in a way analogous to the manner in which God is hidden in the transcendental structure of our subjectivity.

---

[65] See above, n. 63.
[66] Michael Polanyi, *The Tacit Dimension*.

44

Isn't every denial an affirmation of an unarticulated truth? Isn't every 'No!' an implicit assertion of something one is saying 'Yes' to? Doesn't this suggest that 'Yes' and 'No', are not opposites, but that there is only ever 'Yes' (2 Cor. 1:19).

Everything that exists is *of* God, *from* God, and inherently *oriented towards* God. From quantum entanglement to the merging of galaxies, the cosmos exhibits an intricate web of inextricable co-inherences, all of which are finite expressions of the *Logos* of God.

The hypostatic (personal) inter-penetration of Father, Son and Holy Spirit within the Trinity is the Source and Template for every dimension of created reality.

All created *logoi* ('natures', 'substances', 'essences') are found in the Divine *Logos* 'prior'[67] to their creation *ex nihilo*. Until we apprehend that, from all eternity, we 'live and move and have our being' in God (Acts 17:28), we understand nothing about ourselves or God.

The 'end' is in the 'beginning', and the 'beginning' (*archē*) is in the 'end' (goal, purpose, *telos*). Paradoxically, the *'End'* (purpose) *predetermines* the form and content of all that is in the beginning.

---

[67] See above, n. 50.

The *final* cause' (the 'purpose' or 'aim') of creation is the orchestrating power of all 'material, efficient and formal' causes.[68]

The miracle of 'be-ing' escapes the attention of those preoccupied only with 'beings'. There is no adequate materialist accounting for the existence, form and purpose of anything that is.

Science cannot prove the tacit assumptions of its own enterprise. It is an unscientific neglect of metaphysical reflection to presume otherwise.

Functional pragmatism is possible only when the meta-physical conditions for its possibility are denied or ignored.

The irreducibility of self-consciousness to brain tissue is inherently 'unprovable'. Scientific reductionism presumes a creative intelligence within inert matter that the dust of the earth does not contain.

What is 'knowability'? Why is it that anything is 'knowable' at all? Doesn't our understanding of *anything* presume an *Intelligibility* within nature that makes our own knowledge possible?

---

[68] Aristotle identified four causes as those factors that account for all change and movement in the empirical world: material, efficient, formal, final. This vision of interpenetrating causes and effects, reflected especially in Aristotle's notion of final causality, is crucial for the vision of God and the Christian life outlined here. See Aristotle, *Physics* 194 b17–20; see also *Posterior Analytics* 71 b9–11; 94 a20.

It is an atheistic delusion[69] to reduce 'the real' to measurable matter, without considering its *meta*-physical conditions. The materialist cannot be an enlightened materialist until she becomes a better metaphysician.

The best scientists are those who contemplate the conditions of reason and reality that make science possible. The best scientists know it is unscientific to discount metaphysics.

Purpose precedes production, just as form follows function. Both scientific and mystical savants always 'begin with the End in mind'.[70]

To 'begin with the end in mind' implies that the mind is possessed of a teleological apprehension (*Vorgriff*) transcending the mind itself. The mind can no sooner generate a sense of purpose than a transponder can chart a course for the pilot.

Every scientific revolution begins with a *hypothesis* incongruent with current data.[71] But what is a *hypothesis* other than an *intuitive vision* operating within an established scientific framework?

It's unscientific to believe that science defines the limits of what can be known. No enterprise enjoys self-evident self-justification. The only phenomenon that appears to justify itself is self-transcendence.

---

[69] David Bentley Hart, A*theist Delusions: The Christian Revolution and Its Fashionable Enemies.*

[70] Phrase borrowed from Steven Covey, *The 7 Habits of Highly Effective People.*

[71] Thomas Kuhn, *The Structure of Scientific Revolutions.*

Everything in creation is goal-oriented. Everything moves from potentiality to actuality, from possibility to perfection. Whence comes this in-built 'intentionality' if not from a Source 'other' than itself?

Can any created object produce the *entelechy*[72] that inhabits it? Not according to anyone who, like Aristotle and Aquinas, understands that the Purpose (*Telos*, 'final cause') of anything always *precedes*, in the mind of the maker,[73] its production.

Creation presents itself to us as 'purpose-filled'. Acorns become oaks, tadpoles become frogs. Even sub-atomic particles refuse to be disentangled. Doesn't this suggest creation itself is possessed of something like 'a Mind of its own'?

Physics can no sooner account for 'purpose' in creation than Sherlock Holmes could prove the existence of Arthur Conan Doyle.

Organic systems resist reduction to serendipitously connected parts and functions. Mechanistic materialism fails to explain the flawless fluidity with which 'organisms' grow, operate and develop.

---

[72] **Entelechy** is a Greek term meaning the vital principle that guides the development and functioning of an organism or other system or organization.
[73] Dorothy L. Sayers, *The Mind of the Maker*.

Organic growth reveals a kind of 'algorithm of intentionality' which no analytic judgment can apprehend or appreciate. No collection of dead, inert elements, regardless of how cleverly connected, can, of their own accord, generate life.

The 'coherence' exhibited by every organism in creation cannot be reduced to an analysis of its constituent elements. Every organism 'holds together' through a living synergy greater than the sum of its parts.

What if the 'coherences' we observe in creation are themselves participations in, and manifestations of, a more transcendent 'Mystery of Coherence' in which all organisms 'live and move and have their being' (Acts 17:28)?

Intentionality and intelligence are transcendental phenomena. They possess us, we do not possess them.

Relationality, not randomness, is the heart of organic life. Nothing functions organically in nature without being directed by a prior, higher Intelligence. What's wrong with calling this 'higher intelligence' God?

Inspiring our most abstract philosophical or scientific inquiries is an abiding, albeit implicit, sense of *surprise*. The unrestricted desire of the human mind to know is fueled by the delightfully unsettling awareness of the gratuity of being.

Wisdom is abiding amazement at the unnecessary, yet utterly effulgent, miracle of existence. Scientific analysis easily becomes an inability to see the glorious gestalt of the forest because of the bewildering variety of its trees.

Preoccupation with *what* something is blinds us to the unaccountable fact *that* anything is. Grasping (*Vorgriff*) this fundamental distinction between existence (*esse*) and essence (*essentia*) is the difference between hope and despair.

'The world is charged with the grandeur of God'.[74] Mystical happiness consists in cultivating an abiding *Vorgriff* of the mystery of being.

It's one thing for consciousness to *comprehend* the nature (essence) of existent things, but a greater thing to apprehend (*Vorgriff*) the unoriginated Source (*esse*) of that which science studies.

Analysis occludes, rather than unveils, the *irreducibly gracious* character of being. The *whole* cannot be disassembled into *parts* without the Secret of its transcendent coherence escaping our attention.

All things belong to God, and, in an asymmetrical way, God belongs to all things. For while all created beings participate in God, and even though God is impassible and 'unparticipatable' in Godself, it is nonetheless a function of God's *transcendence*, that God 'belongs to all things' as the immanent, inner, loving *Dynamis* of their existence.

---

[74] Gerard Manley Hopkins, *The Grandeur of God*.

Our minds, hearts, and spirits reach out towards the Infinite as sunflowers to the sky. What is less often recognized - because it is given only as a tacit intuition (*Vorgriff*) - is that the Power within us that reaches out towards the Infinite, *is* the Infinite (God) itself.

We cannot know anything unless we implicitly trust our *capacity* for truth. Even the most insignificant act of intellect presumes an indemonstrable belief in an isomorphic synergy of being and knowing.

Religion often functions like a vehicle stuck in second gear. Religion becomes a grind when it does not shift into a higher and deeper *Vorgriff* of God.

'Openness' to the Infinite is the essence of being human. Our unrestricted openness to being, reflected in our unconditional desires to know and possess, is a fertile receptivity established by God Himself.

Our inherent, structural openness to the Infinite is the image and likeness of God within us. God made us for God so that God could glorify Himself in us, and so we might be deified in the process.

The beginnings of every desire arise from an implicitly envisioned End (or perfection) of such desires. The End for which we yearn is always greater, and eschatologically other than, the objects we think we cannot live without.

The End of every desire is in its beginning, just as the oak is 'in' the acorn. But no created end can satisfy the infinite yearning concealed in our every desire. What we call 'God' is the Source and Satisfaction of every desire.

Our every desire apprehends, without necessarily being able to identify it, a Source of Satisfaction that preexists and inspires it. That Source is 'God' - the Uncreated Light in which all our desires appear and are assuaged.

Our *Vorgriff* of God is also an '*Aufhebung*'.[75] When we apprehend 'God' as the transcendent Horizon toward which our knowing and desiring is drawn, we feel ourselves being '*sublated*', i.e., 'lifted up and carried forward' into a fuller realization within a wider and richer context.

There is no reaching God, whether in this world or the next. God is forever beyond our grasp, yet always immediately present as the implicit Source and Satisfaction of our every desire.

God is the implicit Absolute sought in our every thought and action. God is the pre-apprehended Mystery intended in our mental meanderings. God is the unacknowledged *Telos* of our every action.

---

[75] *Aufhebung* - German term, found most notably in the writings of Hegel, which is often translated as 'sublation'. In its broadest sense, **sublation** describes the process of adopting a 'higher perspective' that preserves, negates, and perfects previous, more restrictive interpretive frameworks.

Every negation is an affirmation unaware of itself. Every complaint is an intuition of a solution, every criticism presumes a truth that is beyond criticism.

Everything is of God and from God, and anything that appears to be missing is God humbly accommodating Himself to the capacity of, and for the fulfillment of, those to whom something appears amiss.

God is hidden in plain sight as 'the Term and the Source of the transcendence in and through which' we exist, and which constitutes our essence as subjects and persons.[76]

Anyone who says, definitively, 'there is no truth' tacitly affirms this assertion as true, thus proving himself to be a liar. At the same time, it reveals him in possession of a truth of which he himself is not aware.

To bemoan anything is already to have risen beyond it. Just as unsolicited advice is covert criticism, so also is overt complaining an implicit affirmation of an ecstasy essential to our constitution as self-transcending creatures.

---

[76] *Rahner Foundations of Christian Faith*, 21.

When we say, with St. Augustine, that 'God is closer to us than we are to ourselves',[77] we mean that spiritual vision is identical with the awareness that our capacity for self-awareness is a participation in, and epiphany of, God's self-presencing within us.

Being 'thought by God' is ontologically prior to our desire to think *of* God. Our interest in God is eternally preceded by God's love of us (1 Jn. 4:10).

The more we know, the more we want to know. The insatiability of our hunger and thirst for beauty, goodness and truth *is* the life of God within us, as well as an indication that 'our lives are hidden with Christ in God' (Col. 3:3).

Our desire to know the Source of our capacity for self-presencing is already a participation in that Source. 'God' is the ineffable Power generating both our self-transcendence and our desire to understand it.

To seek God is to have tacitly found God. We cannot contemplate or imagine anything that is not already a participation in the self-communication of God.

The person in search of God is like the mouse in search of the cat.[78]

---

[77] St. Augustine, *Confessions*, III, 6, 11.

[78] 'Amiable agnostics will talk cheerfully about 'man's search for God'. To me, they might as well have talked about the mouse's search for the cat'. (C.S. Lewis, *Surprised by Joy*).

We know ourselves *in* and *through* God, but never *as* God. Our *Vorgriff* of God as *That Which* makes self-transcendence possible also makes it impossible for us to identify ourselves with God.

Though 'utterly other' from God, we experience ourselves as *inseparable from* God. God is in us *as* us, and we are in God as 'gods in God'.[79]

Desire is in the heart before it is in the head. Inspirations filtered through thought alone result in intellectual incontinence.

Our inability to annihilate the smallest unit of matter ($E = mc^2$) reveals finitude to be a disclosure of the Infinite. If a geometric 'point' is divisible a*d infinitum*, is this not a manifestation of the Infinite in and through the finite?

Grasping the impossibility of despair, we experience a *Vorgriff* of God. Despair is a covert desire for deliverance which reaches out for a Source of salvation otherwise known as God.

Expressions of anger are symptoms of hurt, symptoms of hurt are aspirations of love, aspirations of love presume an Absolute Good from which anger and hurt are existential, but not ultimate, departures.

---

[79] See above, n. 8.

Vorgriff

We can't know ourselves to be finite without intuitively experiencing the Presence and 'reality' of Infinity. This 'intuitive experience' is a *Vorgriff* of God.

If we assert that reality is limited to sense experience, we have, in some sense, already transcended sense experience. We couldn't *recognize* the limits of finitude without, at least implicitly, enjoying a standpoint beyond the empirical.

The belief that all is limited to sense experience is not possible without a pre-apprehension (*Vorgriff*) of *That Which* has no intrinsic limit. The assertion that consciousness is a function of brain matter presumes a perspective on brain matter that does not come from the brain itself.

No finite existent is self-explanatory. The implications of this truth speak for themselves.

The ultimate depths of our *Vorgriff* is the realization that our lives are 'hidden with Christ in God'. Our *Vorgriff* of God affords us a flash of ecstasy that is a brief unveiling (*apocalypse*) of our final destiny in God.

'To be', for us, is an expression and extension of the great 'I AM' (Ex. 3:17). We are 'they who are' *in* the One who is 'I AM'. This can be known only as a *Vorgriff*.

Apologetics are anathema to those who abide in an intuitive pre-apprehension of the non-existent God (*Vorgriff*). Intellectual constructs, such as those marshaled against a religionist's opponents, are of a piece with the ignorance they seek to defeat.

Our 'original face'[80] is discovered in the 'original experience' (*Vorgriff*) of God as the unconditioned, ever-present, yet utterly ungraspable 'Background' to all phenomenality. There, we intuitively experience ourselves as those who 'live and move and have our being' in God (Acts 17:28).

Our awareness of God as an 'always receding Horizon' that can never be reached (*Vorgriff*) creates in us a certain *Sehnsucht*, i.e., a 'longing', 'desire', 'yearning', or 'craving'. Spiritual awakening occurs when we recognize our *Sehnsucht* as the Presence of '*That*'[81] for *Which* we long.

There is no excuse for muddy philosophical thinking, save for the fact that intellectual obfuscation can occasion a *Vorgriff* of God which academic precision systematically prevents.

Intuitively grasping that our 'longing to understand' is not actually something we 'possess', but something that 'possesses us', is the source and summit of human intellection.

---

[80] A famous Zen koan asks, 'What is your original face, the face you had before you were born?'

[81] *Tat Tvam Asi* ('*You Are That*') [*Chandogya Upanishad*].

57

When we apprehend God as the *groundless Ground* of all that exists, the sacred and the secular coincide. The world itself becomes an 'efficacious sign'[82] of God's transcendent Presence, and every person seems 'full of grace' (Lk. 1:28; cf. Mk. 3:33).

Awareness (*Vorgriff*) of God's Presence eludes our desire to possess it, yet calls us forward into a space of longing wherein It manifests Itself. Holy *desire* is the closest we can ever get to the One who is the 'fulfillment of all desire'.[83]

When we apprehend God as 'the Light in which we see light' (Ps. 36:9), we grasp, as if in darkness, that the whole of creation is 'backlit' by God. This *Vorgriff* makes every dimension of the finite appear as a veiled theophany of God's Presence.

Experiencing God as 'the Limitless Whither' of our inherent restlessness impels our insatiable quest for God. Enlightenment occurs the moment we realize that 'our quest for God' is, in truth, 'God in search of us'.[84]

---

[82] *Efficacious Sign* - a symbol that communicates what it signifies. This term is used in Catholicism to describe the symbolic power of the sacraments.

[83] Ralph Martin, *The Fulfillment of All Desire*.

[84] Idea borrowed from the complementary titles of books by Abraham Heschel: *Man's Quest for God* and *God in Search of Man*.

Part Two

God

WITHIN

CHAPTER FOUR

Presence

The Mystery of Presence is the *Ur-theophany*[85] of God's self-communication. Self-transcendence is synonymous with Presence, yet the *Power* of Presence is a participation in the more foundational, and completely ineffable, Self-Presencing of God.

An infinite, uncreated Light of Presence precedes, and makes possible, every finite act of 'being present'. This 'Light of Presence' is the 'luminous darkness' of God's self-disclosure.

God is tacitly co-known (*Vorgriff*) as the 'infinite Horizon' towards which our unrestricted desires to know and to possess reach. In Presence, this unthematic pre-apprehension of God becomes existentially electric.

---

[85] *Ur-theophany* - The key revelation (manifestation) of God's ineffable Presence.

Presence, as the practice of self-transcendence, allows us to view the insanity of the world with compassion, without gainsaying its obvious evils. Presence sees through the 'myth of redemptive violence',[86] yet 'condemns no one' (Jn. 8:11).

Presence is a participation in the Peace of God. By 'stepping back from' the dialectics, debates and diatribes that confront us daily, we enter a state of grace (blessing, bliss) that affords a practical wisdom from a place far beyond politics.

In self-transcendence (Presence), we realize it's not, '*I think*, therefore I am', but '*I am*, therefore I can think'. Presence is to thinking what God is to the *logoi* of creation.[87]

Presence - the act of 'being present' - is the mystical space in which our pre-apprehension (*Vorgriff*) of God becomes palpable. Presence is an unrestricted appreciation of being in which the graciousness of the non-existent God is intuitively grasped.

God is the unconditioned *Ur-grund* of all that exists. In Presence, we recede from our egoic selves, and become supremely present to an 'other'. In this, we become living icons of God's transcendent and immanent Love.

---

[86] A phrase made famous by Walter Wink. See: https://www2.goshen.edu/~joannab/women/wink99.pdf.
[87] See above, n. 50.

Presence is the portal to Paradise. For those who abide in Presence, death itself is but an icon of, and opportunity for, deeper self-dispossession and surrender to God.

In self-transcendence (Presence), we acquire compassion for ourselves and others. Presence is a participation in the One 'who loved us first' (1 Jn. 4:19).

Self-transcendence (Presence) gives us a genuine love for ourselves, making it possible for us 'to love our neighbor as ourselves' (Mt. 22:39).

Our ability to 'rise above ourselves' in self-transcendence (Presence) is a participation in the Light of Tabor.[88] In self-transcendence, all is bathed in a Love that is not of this world, giving us a share in the all-forgiving, all-accepting, and all-redemptive Nothingness of God.

In Presence, we are doing for others what God is always doing for us, i.e., serving as the Light by which everything is seen, functioning as the ever-expanding Horizon in which others experience themselves as unconditionally known, accepted and loved.

---

[88] **Light of Tabor** - In Eastern Christian theology, *The Light of Tabor* is the light revealed on Mt. Tabor at the Transfiguration of Jesus. It is the uncreated, divine Light by which human beings are deified by the self-communication of God.

Presence is the ideal synergy of divine and human love. Presence is a Power greater than, and in possession of, those who project it. As a human act, Presence is a participation in the Presence of God as Pure Act (*Actus Purus*).

Presence is an *openness to another* that is of a piece with *openness to God*. This is the deeper meaning of 'whatever you do to the least of these, my children, you do unto me' (Mt. 25:46).

Presence is a participation in the Presence of God (Mt. 25:40). Presence is unrestricted openness to the 'other', infused with Divine Wisdom (*Sophia*). Presence is the fertile soil in which God grows 'little flowers'.[89]

Presence - pure Attention[90] - is a supremely divine-human act. Our 'presence' to another person is a participation in the trinitarian Self-Presencing that is the Source of our own capacity for Presence.

In Presence, God is experienced as God-with-us (*Emmanuel*). Presence is where the immanence of the utterly transcendent God shows its face.

---

[89] Phrase made famous by St. Thérèse of Lisieux (The Little Flower).

[90] French eccentric and philosopher, Simone Weil, developed a radical theory of Attention as the best way to approach the ineffable God. See *'Simone Weil's Radical Conception of Attention'*, https://lithub.com/simone-weils-radical-conception-of-attention.

In Presence, we proceed by the 'Way of Unknowing'.[91] Relinquishing our expectations, we open ourselves to the other with the innocence of a child. This pristine posture of receptivity can, like beholding a newborn baby, soften the hardest heart.

In Presence, we intentionally surrender our preconceived ideas of past and future, focusing on what lies immediately before us. Basking in the present moment, we are enveloped in an updraft of ineffable Love.

Presence is the best way to *apprehend* God without *adverting to* God. In 'being present', we experience a Power greater than ourselves which transforms any anodyne situation into something alive with divine light and love.

Mystics are dismissed as heretics for insisting 'we are not human beings having a spiritual experience, but spiritual beings having a human experience'.[92] In Presence, we experience the truth of the mystics.

In Presence, is there any need to name *That Which* 'makes all things new' (Rev. 21:5)?

---

[91] *Apophasis*. See above, n. 12.

[92] See above, n. 64.

Vorgriff

God is tacitly apprehended in every movement of letting go (*Gelassenheit*). Presence is an epiphany of *Gelassenheit*, resplendent with divine Love.

Presence - self-transcendence - is the amniotic fluid of eternal rebirth. Presence is a womb of sacred fertility in which seeds of deification are brought to full term.

'Being present' to another is the human analogue of our *Vorgriff* of God. When we give our undivided attention, we serve as an unrestricted Horizon, and iridescent Light, in which others experience themselves as unconditionally and unaffectedly loved.

We cannot be open to *anything* without being open to *everything*. This unconditioned openness - present in every act of focal attention - is a participation in the Presence of God.

Many there are who open to God, but few there are who know their openness to God as God Himself in possession of them.

Even when we discern that everything is not as it should be, this discernment is a function of our openness to the Infinite. Evil cannot appear as such, save within the infinite Horizon of human and divine Presence.

Nothing better than Presence expresses the unsullied beauty of human consciousness opening to *That Which* is other than itself. Presence is the very mystery of *Emmanuel* (God-with-us) manifesting Himself within us.

The Zen path to enlightenment is 'to have no opinions'. Placing our opinions in the sacred abeyance of Presence, we remove their power to indict, allowing them to furnish us with insight.

Theological wrangling is as foreign to the practice of Presence as law is to grace. Dogmatics and ethical imperatives are irrelevant to those who grasp the process of *theosis*.

In Presence, to observe is to accept, to accept is to embrace, and to embrace is to love.

In Presence, we glimpse the unity of being and time. In Presence (self-transcendence), we experience God as the 'Power of the Now'.[93]

Our existence in God never is not, because it is never not Now.

Just as the candle calls for snuffing out when the morning sun has appeared, so the need to discuss, argue or persuade dissolves when the light of Presence has arisen.

---

[93] Title of a book by Eckhart Tolle.

For a written or spoken reflection to exhibit any real 'authority' (cf. Mt. 7:29), it must be as prophetic as it is philosophical. Philosophy is only the 'love of wisdom' when it shimmers with prophetic Presence.

In Presence, we become naturally pan-psychic, i.e., we see that the power of Awareness possessing us is an epiphany of divine illumination, one that also permeates the whole of creation.

Our experience of 'being present' involves a concomitant intuition that everything finite is shot through with, and enriched by, a deifying Presence that precedes and perfects it.

'Presence of mind' is also called 'mindfulness'. Paradoxically, 'mindfulness' is a synonym for 'No Mind'.[94] Both refer to our capacity to transcend, i.e., dis-identify from, the thoughts in our heads.

We are not the ideas in our heads. We are they who intuit *'That Which'* makes thinking possible.

Even in self-transcendence (Presence), we are still ourselves, still possessed of self-consciousness. Presence is a divine Embrace in which we 'come to ourselves' by 'opening ourselves' to that which is 'beyond ourselves'.

---

[94] See Philip Krill, *Mushin: Meditations on Mindfulness.*

Jesus was able to sustain an invariant disposition of Presence, whereas, for us, Presence is experienced as an episodic flash of virginal receptivity, an epiphany of supernal beauty. This is why Jesus is God and we are not.

In Presence, we become theophanically one with God. In Presence, we are possessed of God such that we, like the burning bush in the desert, are 'consumed but not destroyed' (Ex. 3:2).

In Presence, we become penetrated with divine glory. Like St. John of the Cross' log in fire,[95] we become incandescent with the 'consuming fire' (Heb. 12:29) of God's divinizing Love.

Presence makes possible a new 'hypostatic union' - not of the two natures of Christ 'united without confusion' - but of ourselves, united with God in a deifying epiphany of transfiguring Love.

Presence is an unconditional openness in which a 'Power greater than ourselves' takes possession of us. That 'Power' is the Presence of God.

Presence is that mystical space in which knower and known are enveloped in a holy communion. In Presence, we experience a powerful *Vorgriff* of God's trinitarian Love.

---

[95] *The Ascent of Mount Carmel*, II, 5, 6; *The Living Flame of Love*, I, 4, 19-24.

Presence is the Paschal Mystery in action. In Presence, we die to our false selves and rise as our true selves. In Presence, we participate in the death and resurrection of God's Eternal Word.

The experience of Presence always strikes us as an event of 'salvation'. Presence is an epiphany (*Vorgriff*) in which we feel as if we have been set free from artificial identities, and ushered into a world where our lives are constituted by a Power greater than ourselves.

In Presence, we intuitively perceive that 'we are thought' before 'we think'. In Presence, we experience ourselves as 'hearers of a Word'[96] that is beyond human articulation.

The experience of self-transcendence involved in any act of Presence brings an automatic sense of bliss and peace. Presence promises an ever-greater depth of joy to those who surrender ever-more completely to it.

Every moment of Presence - i.e., conscious self-transcendence - portends a unification with, and deification within, the 'peace that passes all understanding' (Phil. 4:7).

The glory of God can be glimpsed in every moment of pure Attention.[97] The instant we open to any person or situation before us, the beauty of the Trinity flashes forth.

---

[96] See Karl Rahner, *Hearer of the Word: Laying the Foundation for a Philosophy of Religion*.
[97] See above, n. 90.

God is apprehended as the 'Power of Now'.[98] Yet, 'God' is as unfindable and indefinable as is every present (and vanishing) moment.

Eternity is found in the epicenter of the present moment. Nothing exists apart from Now, just as nothing exists outside of God. In Presence, these truths are mystically understood.

'Being present' is the actualization of self-transcendence, which is itself the image and likeness of God within us. In Presence, Divine Love possesses us, divinizes us, and bathes us in a Light the world cannot comprehend (Jn. 1:5).

There is no better space than that of 'letting go' (*Gelassenheit*) to apprehend the Presence of God. God is discerned in the momentary *delight* arising whenever we 'give up' trying to control anyone or anything.

'Now' is the infinitely divisible point that is no 'where' and every 'where'. 'Now' is the indefinable nexus that has no 'when' and no 'then'. Can we now see how the 'Now' is the habitation of the non-existent God?

Sanctity consists in continually refreshing the 'Power of Now' within self-consciousness. We come alive when we are fully present to the Power of the present moment.

[98] See above, n. 93.

Practicing 'being present' is both a gift and a task. In Presence, our inherent nature as self-transcendent is actualized and perfected.

Those who live entirely in the Now have neither regrets nor forebodings. They experience a moment-by-moment deliverance from the grief and guilt caused by too much thinking.

The only time is Now. Living in the Now, we experience God in real time.

Is it possible to be simultaneously urgent and unruffled, or driven and detached? Yes, if our self-awareness is established in Presence, which is our participation in the *Shekinah* of God.[99]

Every moment of *chronos* (chronological time) becomes a moment of *kairos* (perfect timing) whenever the power of Now is felt with full force.

Presence is an epiphany of God whose Spirit creates the space of 'letting be' in which both divine and human persons experience transcendent, holy communion.

---

[99] *Shekinah* - an English transliteration of a Hebrew word meaning 'dwelling' or 'settling' and denotes the Presence of God. This concept is found in the Torah, as mentioned in Exodus 25:8.

Acts of internal surrender (*Gelassenheit*) can go on *ad infinitum*. As the mind empties, 'water will spring from us as from the source of eternity'.[100]

God is intuitively experienced in every act of letting-go (*Gelassenheit*), especially when we let go of our ideas of God. In the act of 'letting go', the Presence of God manifests Itself.

We cannot be holier than we actually are. Holiness is a humble acceptance of who we are *as* we are.

Presence is an act of acceptance that issues, effortlessly and organically, in such moral improvements necessary for the full flourishing God desires for each of us.

In the depths of our being, it is impossible to *simplify* too much. When we 'reduce by half'[101] every moment of 'letting go', we asymptotically approach perfect union with God.

Simplicity itself is the prime sign that we are living the 'sacrament of the present moment'.[102] 'Downsizing' becomes irresistible once we have discovered Presence to be 'the one thing needful' (Lk. 10:42).

---

[100] Angelus Silesius, *The Cherubic Pilgrim*.

[101] An epigram of Soshu Koichi Tohei Sensei, Aikido master and founder of the Ki Society.

[102] See Jean-Pierre Caussade, *The Sacrament of the Present Moment*.

Vorgriff

When we see ourselves *diminishing* - say from serious illness or old age - we also apprehend, by way of *Vorgriff*, our immortality. Our ability to *notice* our own dissolution reveals our deepest, deathless identity.

The fact that we can never know ourselves as we are known by God (cf. 1 Cor. 8:3; 13:12) is an invitation to surrender to God in a sustained act of childlike trust. Such is our sharing in the *kenosis* of Christ who, even as God, knows 'the Father is greater than I' (Jn. 14:28).

The mystical depths of religion open when we recognize the limits of religious routines. Religious formation, at some indefinable inflection point, becomes the enemy of spiritual *transformation*.

Weariness is God's instrument for spiritual awakening. When the 'pain of holding on' becomes greater than the 'pain of letting go', we let go. Therein lies the peace of God.

Because Presence is the image and likeness of God within us, Christ is *compelled* to call each of us his 'mother, brother and sister' (Mk. 3:35). The risen Christ shows Himself to us in every act of self-transcendence.

Because our capacity for Presence (self-transcendence) is the divinely created essence of being human, Christ also says that 'whatever you do to anyone, you do me' (cf. Mt. 25:46).

Presence is the power of God, made visible in Christ, in which all things are 'made new' (Rev. 21:5).

Our lives are fulfilled when we become incandescent with the Life of God. The *Fiat* of Mary - 'Let it be done to me as You desire' (Lk. 1:38) - is the singular means of deification.

The universality of asceticism reveals a passion for simplicity that is born of, and reflects, the Presence of God. Every impulse to 'simplify' is an inspiration from the God who 'empties Himself' in the Incarnation and creation.

True asceticism means dissolving every image of ourselves and of God other than the apprehension that 'we are' because 'God is'.

To approach God as No-thing, we must divest ourselves of everything that is not God, including our ideas about God. Perpetual *relinquishment*, physical and spiritual, is the 'narrow way' (Mt. 7:13-14) into the kingdom of God.

The transcendent God is always at work, pulling us out of our earthly attachments into the naked Now. Presence reveals every moment to be our eternal habitation.

Holiness consists in cultivating a never-ending spirit of *deconstruction*. Perpetual *divestment* is the best investment in our relationship with God.

We experience the Presence of God in our willingness to *know nothing* of God. In every instant of 'letting go', especially of our ideas of God, the Holy Spirit refreshes our souls.

Cultivating an interior posture of 'allowing' turns us into another 'mother of God' (cf. Mk. 3:33). In our openness to everyone and everything, we are possessed of God in a divine synergy of consent and conception (Lk. 1:38).

Purity of heart means acquiring, and sustaining, an inner sense of ever-deepening detachment. In Presence, we detach from ourselves and open ourselves to the Infinite.

Apprehension of self-transcendence is the existential equivalent of being 'born from above' (Jn. 3:7). When we 'observe' ourselves, we 'rise above' ourselves. This 'higher self' is also our 'deepest self', known in its fullness only by God (Col. 3:3; Rev. 2:17).

Every denial of self-transcendence is its affirmation. To *deny* anything is to affirm a higher perspective, which itself presumes a higher 'self'. Our capacity for self-*transcendence* is also an affirmation of our divine-human identity.

Self-transcendence is not an escape from self, but a revelation of a 'self' that can never escape itself. It is also a 'self' which, because of its teleological orientation to its Source (God), remains a mystery to itself (Col. 3:3; Rev. 2:17).

We experience joy and peace when we 'rise above' ourselves in Presence. In Presence, we are *already seated* with Christ at the Father's right hand' (Eph. 2:6; Col. 3:1).

Those who abide in self-transcendence (*Presence*) acquire expanded patience for themselves and others. They realize that the apex of holiness is humility.

Those who have developed their capacity to 'step back from themselves' in Presence know that *forgiveness* is the inner structure of being human. Presence is the space of self-transcendence in which all things are reconciled in Christ.

Self-transcendence (Presence) *is* self-forgiveness. As soon as we 'get over' ourselves, we are empowered to love and forgive others (Mt. 22:39).

We possess ourselves only when we 'transcend' ourselves. Otherwise, we 'lose ourselves' in unselfconscious interactions with the people, places and things of our daily lives.

Our capacity for self-transcendence is discovered in our failures and regrets. When we say, 'I wish I had not done that!', we discover 'the true me', unmarred by the mistakes we make.

To experience our limitations is already to have transcended them. We can neither embrace nor bemoan our finite condition without having already risen 'above', and 'beyond', it.

Because we are transcendental subjects, we are capable of recognizing, respecting and/or rejecting our sense experience. Only spiritual beings are capable of recognizing their irreducibility to matter.

When we know God to be as intimately present as he is utterly unknowable, we lose our propensity to compare, criticize or condemn. In Presence, we understand that 'God's ways are not our ways' (Isa. 55:8), and we instinctively know not to judge (Mt. 7:1).

Self-consciousness is a *transcendental* experience. When we become aware of ourselves as *capable of* Presence, we realize that this 'awareness of awareness'[103] could go on forever. Herein lies our *Vorgriff* of God.

What is involved in the simple act of 'taking time'? Who, we might ask, is the one who 'takes his time'? Are there two of us? Are they both 'real'?

When we 'take our time', or 'take ourselves lightly',[104] we 'stand outside ourselves', 'giving ourselves' the space and the freedom to 'assess ourselves' and perhaps 'change ourselves'. *Whence* comes this capacity for self-assessment, re-adjustment and change?

---

[103] Rupert Spira, *Being Aware of Being Aware*.

[104] 'Angels can fly because they take themselves lightly' (G.K. Chesterton, *Orthodoxy*).

Apprehending the infinite Horizon of self-transcendence in Presence is the heavenly alternative to living in hell, i.e., in a rootless, mechanized world, lacking purpose and containing a coherence it cannot explain.

Our experience of 'being able to observe ourselves' intimates a Source of self-transcendence that is both one with, and greater than, what we call our usual 'self'.

God perfects self-consciousness by calling us beyond ourselves in self-transcendence. Self-transcendence (Presence) is the space of the Spirit where our divinization occurs.

If, in Presence, we know our 'participative oneness' with God, we will experience the miracle of *theosis* (deification). In Presence, self-transcendence becomes self-possession.

Presence is where we experience the inner meaning of the patristic maxim, 'God became man so man could become God'.[105] Presence is where the *Logos* of God fulfills the longing of man.

Unlike fish, who are congenitally unaware of the water they swim in, we are gifted with 'knowing' the unknowable God, whose knowledge of us is the condition for the possibility of knowing ourselves.

---

[105] See above, n. 48.

The irreducibility of our 'I' is ecstasy for the saint, but agony for those lacking in self-awareness. Suicide is a search for self-transcendence under a cloud of despair.

There is no need to despair, and every reason to dance, once the 'I' who says, 'I can't stand to live with myself' awakens to the fact that the 'I' who is speaking is the savior of the 'I' who 'can't stand to live with itself any longer'.

Our ability to predicate anything about ourselves reveals us to ourselves in a way that is beyond predication.

Once we step outside ourselves into self-transcendence, we stop 'crowding' others. Covetousness and envy dissolve in the space of Presence.

God is found in the 'pause' and the 'step back'. Whenever we call 'Time out!' from the craziness of life, we step out of time and into the kingdom of God.

We are *of* God and *from* God, and it is God Himself, in us *as* us, who is the Source and Satisfaction of our irrepressible self-transcendence.

If we don't see God in the self-transcendent structure of knowing and desiring, we shan't see God at all. God's Spirit is embedded with ours in our inherent Openness to what is other than ourselves.

Self-transcendence is a trajectory that leads directly into the heart of the Trinity.

It's not so much that we possess self-transcendence; it's not even that we are possessed *of* self-transcendence. It's that we are possessed *by* self-transcendence.

Our very ability to 'rise above' ourselves is, in truth, God saving us from ourselves and revealing our unbreakable union with Him.

We are possessed of self-transcendent consciousness, which is God's own self-transcending Self possessing us. The 'I' with which we see God is the same 'I' with which God sees us.[106]

My mother used to say, 'You don't know what to do with yourself, do you?' Why did it take me 65 years to hear the bliss-filled promise of self-transcendence in her words?

If I say, 'I don't know what to do with myself', who is the 'I' who doesn't know what to do with himself? Are there two of me? Is only one of them real? How can I know?

---

[106] Paraphrase of Meister Eckhart's famous quote, 'The eye through which I see God is the same eye through which God sees me; my eye and God's eye are one eye, one seeing, one knowing, one love'. *Sermon, 'True Hearing'.*

Through a deeper apprehension of self-transcendence as a participation in the triune God, we can see that the contradictions and chaos in the foreground of our perception are ultimately reconciled in the supernatural Background constituting that same self-transcendence.

In willing to become 'strangers to ourselves', we discover ourselves. Letting go of self-understanding, we experience self-transcendence. In experiencing self-transcendence, we experience our ontological union with, as well as our 'otherness from', God.

No conceptualization can capture, or adequately describe, our 'original experience of self-presence'.[107] When we attempt to make this original experience of self-presence explicit, an even more original epiphany of self-presence is constellated, this time in a way that shows itself to precede and transcend our attempts at explication.

'The original experience of self-presence' is always immediate and absolute. It cannot be grasped, only apprehended. It *grasps us*, we don't 'grasp 'it'.

Awakening to self-transcendence is an ever-fresh epiphany of divine revelation. Presence never grows old, yet it forever exceeds our ability to express it.

---

[107] Karl Rahner, *Foundation of Christian Faith*, 14-23.

Just as God the Father is Himself insofar as he generates the perfect reflection of Himself in his Son, so we come to a knowledge of ourselves insofar as we find ourselves mirrored in the faces of our models. At the same time, we cannot know ourselves as God knows us (Col. 3:3) simply by touching our faces in these mirrors.

No philosophical term can describe the unfathomable mystery of human *personhood*. Even 'personhood' is an impoverished way of pointing to the primordial 'who' that each of us is. 'Who' we are can never be reduced to 'what' we are.

No one can speak for God who does not do so in their own voice. Only from one's own hidden identity in God (Col. 3:3) do words of wisdom emerge. [108]

Ego, not personality, dissolves within the virginal point (*Le Point Vierge*)[109] of our being. God has always known us only as 'me' and 'you', even if the egoic-pursuit of 'me' and 'you' estranges us from our true selves.

---

[108] This is the meaning of the Vedantic phrase, '*Atman* (soul) is *Brahman* (God)'. The individual soul is asymmetrically co-inherent with its Source. See above, n. 23.
[109] **Le Point Vierge** is a phrase popularized by Thomas Merton (*Conjectures of a Guilty By-Stander*) to describe 'a point of nothingness at the center of our being which is untouched by sin and by illusion, a point of pure truth, a point or spark which belongs entirely to God, which is never at our disposal, from which God disposes of our lives ... This little point of nothingness and of absolute poverty is the pure glory of God in us'. It is worth noting that Merton fastened on his concept by reading and corresponding with the Catholic Islamic scholar, Louis Massignon.

Vorgriff

Contra *Advaita*,[110] we experience an irreducible singularity and personal uniqueness in the experience of Presence. When we 'go beyond ourselves' and become, in Presence, the 'observer' of ourselves, we discover our 'true' selves, albeit in an intuitive, fleeting manner.

It's impossible to escape the irreducibly unique person each of us is. I can never not be 'me', even (especially?) when I say that 'I' do not exist. We never cease being ourselves, whether here or in eternity.

In self-transcendence, we experience others and the world in a space of 'bare Attentiveness', devoid of analysis or interpretation. We are never more 'ourselves' than in the space of pure Presence.

Even when we question our own judgments, it is still 'us' doing it. Elusive as it is, we always experience a pre-apprehension (*Vorgriff*) of self-transcendence, even (especially?) when we recognize our limitations as human beings.

Our 'true self' is untouched and untouchable by what the world calls 'sin'. Our capacity to acknowledge that we have made mistakes is proof positive that there is more to us than any number of missteps can affect.

---

[110] *Advaita* is a form of idealist monism, according to which the world has no separate existence apart from God [*Brahman*], the ultimate, transcendent and immanent Source of all that is. *Advaita* finds expression in the anonymous Hindu verse, '*Brahman* [God] is alone True, and this world of plurality is an error; the individual self is not different from *Brahman* [God]'.

Sin and suffering are 'allowances' by God to awaken us to our true identity in Presence. Every fault is a 'happy fault',[111] since our ability to acknowledge our faults as such reveals us, *au fond*, to be faultless.

It is said, 'Hate the sin, but love the sinner'. Wouldn't it be better to say: 'Love the sin which awakens the sinner to his sinless identity' or 'Love the one who, in confessing her sins, has already transcended them'?

There is no 'if' in God. If more preachers knew this, their churches would not be imploding.

Where God's 'if-less' love is denied, all hell breaks loose.

God, as Pure Act (*Actus Purus*), in Whom essence and attributes are identical, does not will 'consequently' what He did not will 'antecedently'. If any are 'left behind', whether on earth or in hell, God is to blame.

Isn't it interesting that our own instincts for forgiveness often exceed those we attribute God? Why do many feel obliged to question God's eschatological annihilation of sinners if not because of a deeper intuition of God as Love disclosed in Christ?

---

[111] 'O happy fault that earned so great, so glorious a Redeemer!' *Exultet*. See: https://www.usccb.org/prayer-worship/liturgical-year/easter/easter-proclamation-exsultet.

Forgiveness is a divine grace given and received the moment a sin is recognized and acknowledged. Relief arises *the instant* we realize we have gone wrong. Realizing we are lost finds us immediately back at the place where we can make a fresh start.

The miracle of Presence is no less mysterious and happily disconcerting as that of existence itself. For whence comes the fact that the structural givenness of the world is isomorphically synergized with our desire and ability to comprehend it?

Awareness of our own awareness is as mystifying and exhilarating as the uncanniness of being itself. Could anything be more intuitively clear than that our 'knowing' and 'that which is to be known' are made for each other?

Our ability to *notice* that we are possessed of an unrestricted desire to know is itself a *trans*-rational power (*dynamis*). Our capacity for Presence is greater than our ability to think, more primordial than analysis, and ontologically prior to our penchant for epistemic inquiry.

Those who live and rest in the transcendental 'I' have no need to explain or defend. Everything they do or say is done to *express*, not to impress.

Those who know God as No-thing wish to be one with God in perpetual, personal diminishment. Presence is the impoverishment of everything but 'the one thing necessary' (Lk. 10:42).

We can 'face ourselves' in a merciful, not malicious, way when we have shed the masks we have acquired trying to 'face the world'. The 'I' with which we see ourselves is an eternal 'self', identical with the 'me' God has loved since 'before the foundation of the world' (Eph. 1:4).

At the heart of the deified life is an abiding awareness of the immanence of the transcendent God. In Presence, we know that God Himself is the Source and Satisfaction of our desire for God.

Mystics experience their desire for God as the actual Presence of God possessing them.

It is metaphysically significant that we can't see our own faces, save in a mirror. The 'I' who sees most clearly is interior to the 'I' who sees through the eyes. If the eyes are the window to the soul, the soul is the Light in the window.

In the virginal point (*Le Point Vierge*)[112] of our being, we are as alive and unselfconscious as a child.

---

[112] See above, n. 109.

In Presence, we discern a *hiatus* between our 'features' and the 'I' that transcends those 'features'. In Presence, a kind of salvific *satori*[113] arises in which we awaken to ourselves as those whose lives 'are hidden with Christ in God' (Col. 3:3).

The 'self' that is capable of transcending itself is faceless, yet exquisitely personal. Our deepest identity - the ultimate 'who' each of us - is known only by God.

Artificial Intelligence (AI) is incapable of first-person self-consciousness, no matter how cleverly programmed to mimic it. Making AI empirically indistinguishable from self-transcendence does not make it identical. Digital duplication is not spiritual replication.

Our innate capacity, and unstoppable propensity, to 'rise above' whatever besets us is the Life of God within us. God is One with us, drawing us beyond ourselves into the very Mystery that inspires and sustains us.

Systems suffocate, but never entirely. Our capacity for self-transcendence breaks the seal on all confining definitions of being human. Our irreducible subjectivity allows us to escape the coffin of death-dealing ideologies.

---

[113] **Satori** - a Japanese Buddhist term for 'awakening', 'comprehension', 'understanding', 'enlightenment'.

There is nothing we cannot wonder about, most especially ourselves. Our capacity to contemplate our own self-transcendence intimates the infinite depths of who we are in God.

In Presence, we experience God in us *as* us. We are *living icons* of the triune, self-transcending God, even as God is the unfathomable Source of our capacity for self-transcendence.

Our desire for God - and therefore our love of God - is irrepressible. Nothing we do can destroy, or in the smallest way damage, the 'pearl of great price' (Mt. 13:46) which we are.

Is our self-awareness a direct perception of ourselves, or does it originate from Elsewhere? Is the power of Presence a participation in the self-presencing of God? If so, how are we to imagine this 'participation'?[114]

The key to mystical knowledge is this: we are possessed *of* the very God who possesses us.

Hope springs eternal because, in the depths of our being, we experience ourselves as persons of infinite possibility. A horizon of unlimited promise grows wider, yet ever less reachable, the further we advance into Presence.

---

[114] See above, n. 20.

Our capacity for joy is without limit, and actualizes itself when we abide in the *dynamis* of self-transcendence. In Presence, we experience an epiphany of God's eternal glory.

Self-transcendence is a participation in the theandric[115] mystery of Christ. Our ability to become 'observers of our selves' is a participation in the triune self-presencing of God.

Presence is an experience of the risen Christ who, in Presence, imparts a share in the divine-human synergy subsisting in Him as God's' Eternal Word.

Seeing our lives *diminish* with time reveals a timeless identity at the center of our being. Watching the 'dying of our light', we are illumined with a greater, hidden Light within.

Our capacity for self-transcendence is a participation in the Mystery of God. The fact this truth can be asserted but never rationally demonstrated only proves the point.

Our transcendental orientation to God, disclosed in Presence, *is* the Presence of God within us. This suggests that, at some fundamental level, nature and grace are one, and, ultimately, 'nature' is 'graced' all the way down.

---

[115] *'Theandric'* - 'God-human'. Theologically, *'theandric'* refers to those actions of Christ in which he used the human nature as an instrument of his divinity.

Every 'this' or 'that' we assert of ourselves enjoys no ontological reality in the 'I' that each of us is. In Presence, we experience ourselves as a 'mystery', inaccessible to our understanding and impervious to our predications.

Thinking is an expression of consciousness, not its definition. Our capacity for Presence (self-transcendence) is prior to, and independent of, our mental exercises.

As spiritual beings possessed of an *apriori* openness to being, nothing can estrange us from ourselves, nothing can threaten our receptivity to God. Self-transcendence is perfected in Presence.

The existential apprehension (*Vorgriff*) of God experienced in Presence reveals faith as more essentially human than knowledge. Discrete knowing transpires *within* an infinite Horizon of Intelligibility that can only be trusted, never explicitly known.

Laughter is living proof that none of the labels we put on ourselves limit our creative capacity. Because we can always ask questions, every 'explanation' is but another invitation for deeper exploration.

Reflective writings, such as these, have 'life' only to the extent they radiate Presence. In Presence, we experience an 'intuition' (*Vorgriff*) of the Source of our own self-transcendence.

CHAPTER FIVE

Pretence

Obtuseness is the 'sin within the sin'. It's one thing to offend another, but a more intractable sin to remain oblivious to the offense.

Cluelessness bespeaks a moral malady more deadly than ethical invidiousness.

Ethics is what religionists substitute for experiential knowledge of God. Morality is the default position of those who are invincibly ignorant of God's omnipresence.

The perfection of ethics is the dissolution of the deliberative (*gnomic*) will.[116] Just as a musical virtuoso has no need of a libretto, the deified person, like Christ Himself, has no need of directives to do the truth co-naturally.

Failing a *Vorgriff* of our unity-in-difference with God, ethics, as a set of rules for right relationship with God, are nothing other than tools of ignorance.

Freedom is not the capacity to choose between good and evil, but the inability to do evil.

Astonishment at the *fact* of existence is the spontaneous human response to the primordial act of why-less Love that makes existence possible. Problems disappear when we sustain a state of awe and gratitude.

---

[116] **Gnomic Will** - The concept of the gnomic, or deliberative, will is a central point in the Christology of St. Maximus the Confessor (580-662). According to Maximus, if human nature required the real capacity freely to reject God, then Christ could not have been fully human. Christ, however, *is* fully human and fully *free*. He possesses no *gnomic* (deliberative) will because his will was perfectly *free* from the need to deliberate or decide between right or wrong, truth or error, good or evil. Thus, any true human being cannot be said to have the 'capacity' for sin. Rather, our capacity to sin must be at most a privation of being properly human, a deficiency whose ultimate disappearance would - far from hindering the human will - free human nature from a sick and alien condition. What distinguished Christ in this regard from the rest of humanity, if Christological orthodoxy is to be believed, is not that he lacked a kind of freedom that all other human beings possess, but that he was not subject to the kinds of extrinsic constraints upon his freedom (ignorance, delusion, corruption of the will, and so forth) that enslave the rest of us. Christ was - as we should all wish to become - incapable of any deviation from the Good. Christ had a perfect knowledge of the Good and was thus perfectly rational. As a fully human being, Christ could not sin; hence, he alone among men was fully free.

The *Logos* of Heraclitus is at odds with the *Logos* of God.[117] The logic of 'might makes right',[118] is insanity for those whose interior vision is acclimated to a *Vorgriff* of God.

Because we are 'gods in God'[119] and 'lights from Light' (Mt. 5:14), we are both indestructibly good and invincibly ignorant. Our inherent goodness as God's 'image and likeness' (Gen. 1:26) is ontologically matched with our inability to grasp the Mystery of God as the *Archē* (Origin, Source) of our existence.

Guilt and shame masquerade as conscience before we appropriate our *Vorgriff* of God. To intuit God as *Actus Purus* is also to experience purity of heart as our true identity in God.

Within our *Vorgriff* of God, we realize evil is a function, and fruit, of human ignorance, yet we are freed from harboring animosity towards ourselves or others. Our apprehension (*Vorgriff*) of God is empty of accusation, even as we see evil for what it is.

Hell is the inability to perceive God's Presence in every act of human knowing, willing, and doing.

---

[117] The *Logos* of Heraclitus is, 'War is the father of all...the king of everything' (*Fragment* 53). The *Logos* of God is Christ, the forgiving victim. See René Girard, *Things Hidden Since the Foundation of the World,* chapter 4.

[118] Words of Thrasymachus in Plato's *Republic,* Book I, Section 3.

[119] See above, n. 8.

Darkness is not the opposite of Light, and evil is not the opposite of good. Darkness, evil, and Satan represent the *absence* of something Good, and an *'absence'* is never a 'something'. The reification of evil is of a piece with evil itself.

Satan is not the opposite of God, any more than darkness is the opposite of light. God is 'light in whom there is no darkness' (1 Jn. 1:5). Lucifer, the angel of darkness, is, despite his fall from grace, still a Light-bearer of God.[120]

Just as the 'Father of lights declares darkness to be his creature' (Ezk. 32:8; Jas. 1:17), God uses his fallen angel, Lucifer ('Light-bringer'), to enlighten us, so that, when, falling into the pig sty of our sins, we 'come to our senses' and 'return to the house of our Father' (Lk. 15:17-18).

God has no equal, and goodness has no evil twin. Until we see that darkness is but the *absence of light*, we remain in the same darkness that the Light of Christ has already overcome (Jn. 1:5).

Satan's desire to 'reign in hell rather than serve in heaven'[121] is, in its own way, a desire *for* heaven. No one, not even Satan, can hold out forever without becoming aware that the presuppositions of rebellion are, in truth, aspirations for God.

---

[120] 'Lucifer' means 'Light-bringer'.
[121] John Milton, *Paradise Lost*, I. 263.

Every hatred is love unaware of itself. When 'kicking against the goad' (Acts 26:14) is unveiled as a desire for Absolute Good, the kicking and the goading stop.

The tacit *telos* of all testiness is an aspiration for eternal Ecstasy, which, in actuality, is a desire for God. Resentment is an *inverse desire* for divine reconciliation.

Every objection contains a covert affirmation. Miserable people remain so long as they fail to perceive their own desire for mercy embedded in their protestations.

The conflation of 'why' and 'how' - i.e., the collapse of the 'final and formal causes' with the 'material' and 'efficient' causes - is the birth (and death) of scientific materialism. A purpose-less anything is found nowhere.

Reductionists aspire to *negative transcendence.* They seek the divine in *deconstruction.* They seek to overcome the world by subdividing it into a million little, self-explanatory pieces.

Are we destined to lose our child-like sense of the intimate otherness of things? Must we necessarily allow our habits to replace our in-built sense of wonder? If so, the world is doomed.

Sin is blindness to the world as a sacrament of God's Love. Sin is a radical empiricism that conflates depth with breadth, and meaning with inert matter.

Wisdom is a blessed awareness of the *'such-ness'* of things. *Knowledge* is an ever-evolving understanding of the *'how-ness'* of things. Knowledge is to Wisdom as velvet art is to the Mona Lisa.

Sin is a glorification of the utilitarian, and a sacralizing of the secular. Such reductionism stimulates envy, making it impossible to experience a *Vorgriff* of God.

Purity of heart and *interior freedom* redound organically to those who allow themselves to be grasped by a *Vorgriff* of God.

The only 'unforgivable sin' (Mk. 3:29) is the unwillingness to forgive. Yet, even this sin is forgiven the moment we forgive those unwilling to forgive.

If we don't apprehend the teleological (purpose-driven) nature of all things, the universe becomes a collection of infinitely re-arrangeable objects - a world that promises unlimited creativity and control, but which delivers suicidal *ennui*.

Not to be *enchanted* by the 'intuition of being' is to remain oblivious to the most enthralling and ecstatic experience a person can have.

Sin is the absence of self-consciousness. We are bulls in a china shop until we discover ourselves as capable of, and called to, not breaking things.

Sin is spiritual stupidity, and the greatest spiritual stupidity is to believe sin could ever separate us from the love of God incarnate in Christ Jesus (Rom. 8:38-39).

Self-consciousness is neither an illusion nor a epiphenomenon. Science shows itself to be unscientifically stupid when it asserts that our inherent self-transcendence is a function of, rather than the foundation of, the machinations of cerebral tissue.

The mind is as determinative of our thoughts as a radio is to the frequencies it transmits. Thoughts come *through* the brain and inspirations arise *in* the heart, not as generated by inert body tissues.

Consciousness is *permitted*, not *emitted*, by the brain. This is just another way of saying, 'The soul is the *form* of the body'.[122]

It is our 'forgetfulness of being' that is the root cause of our violence towards nature and others. When God is not grasped as the groundless Ground of existence, we idolize beings and imagine ourselves as stand-alone 'gods'.

---

[122] St. Thomas Aquinas, *Summa Theologica*, Part I, Q75.

Shame has no place in God, nor in those who abide in God. Shame is the default position of those who know God only by hearsay.

Guilt has no place in the lives of those who know God, save as a warning sign that our alignment with God is slightly off kilter.

Guilt functions in the lives of a saint like the lane departure system in a car. It serves as course correction to get us more perfectly aligned on the highway to heaven.

Mystics travel to heaven as if in self-driving cars, needing no lane alerts to arrive at their pre-programmed destination.

Prophetic words find no purchase in the 'economy of antagonism', which is the world's default position. The grammar of God is a stumbling block for geopolitical logic.

Irresponsibility is impossible for the self-transcending subject. Every attempt to disavow responsibility makes the objector the owner of his own disavowal.

The world is an interdependent network of interlocking polarities which the sinful self perceives as dichotomous and divisive. God establishes 'otherness' and 'alterity' as divine *excellences*, yet we turn them into antagonisms and antinomies.

'*What* something is' is *nothing* in comparison with the inexplicable fact '*that* it is'. The failure to discern, contemplate, and abide in this unbridgeable metaphysical abyss is the source of the world's ills.

The joy of the saint is incomprehensible to those who know only a conceptualized God. Ecstasy, as our 'natural' state of being in our Original Unity[123] with God, is a pipe dream to all who do not know God as the *immanent Source* of all that exists.

We *are* before we are *this* or *that*. Bliss arises naturally when we recognize ourselves as ontologically prior to any definition or description we can give of ourselves.

Eternal life is to know ourselves to be *of* God, *in* God, and *through* God. God Himself awakens us to our derivative, yet ontologically real, 'participation' in, the life of God.

It is *God* we are seeking in all our attempts at self-satisfaction. Blinded by our inveterate ignorance (sin), we mistake specific goods for the Transcendent Good (God) which alone can satisfy our hearts' desire.

God establishes 'love' and 'communion' as 'sacraments' of divine unity, but in our hands they become lust and control. No wonder people don't get along.

---

[123] '*Original Unity*' is a term coined by John Paul II to describe our state prior to the 'original sin' of Adam and Eve. See: https://www.vatican.va/content/john-paul-ii/en/audiences/1979/documents/hf_jp-ii_aud_19791107.html.

The actual person that each of us is - the 'I am' that 'is hidden with Christ in God (Col. 3:3) - is as untouchable by sin as it is inaccessible to cognition. The '*who*' that '*I am*' is as much untouched by my sins as it eludes my understanding.

Sin is a series of shifting symptoms of an intractable spiritual disease. This disease is *interior blindness* to our inherent orientation to, and inseparable union with, the Source of our desires.

Mary's *Fiat* will ultimately prove stronger than Herod's slaughter of the innocents.

No problem is solved from within its own frame of reference. The smallest act of self-sacrificial love shows that the theory of 'redemptive violence' is a myth.[124]

'Saving face' is the illusion people adopt 'until we have the faces'.[125] Every attempt to 'save face' is a betrayal of our true identity.

Our ability to 'face ourselves' presumes a perspective on ourselves in which we discover the 'face we had before we were born'[126] Our deepest identity is known only by God (Rev. 2:17), as our lives are 'hidden with Christ in God' (Col. 3:3).

---

[124] See above, n. 86.

[125] C. S. Lewis, *Till We Have Faces: A Myth Retold.*

[126] See above, n. 80

Failure of self-awareness is worse than the actual evils we commit (Lk. 23:34). Lack of situational awareness is more tragic that the messes we create.

Jesus is more exasperated at Philip's denseness (Jn. 14:9) than with Peter's denial (Lk. 22:60-61).

The world is sleep-walking towards Armageddon. History is an on-going nightmare of war from which we cannot awaken. Perhaps Armageddon will cause us to 'come to our senses' (Lk. 15:17)?

Our apprehension (*Vorgriff*) of God leads to the growing awareness that violence is the foundation of human culture. In God's uncreated Light, we see clearly that civilization is established and underwritten by the threat of violence and use of force.[127]

'Those who live by the sword die by the sword' (Mt. 26:52). Why? Because every civilization is 'built on the dissolving sands' (Mt. 7:26-27) of reciprocal violence.

The 'peace the world gives' (Jn. 14:27) is perpetually threatened by fear, and backed up by the threat of force. But, anything built on fear ensures its ultimate demise.

---

[127] The mimetic theory of René Girard. See above, n. 117.

'Might makes right' only in the minds of the morally demented. Evil is the inability to see evil when it's right in front of your face.

Enemies are entwined in a love-hate duet that neither party can live without. The more we attempt to distance ourselves from the dreaded 'other', the more we are defined by the one we loathe.

Mutual hatred turns warring parties into siamese twins.

The world is a matrix of mendacious antinomies blind to its demonic dynamic. Deicide is the world's default position.

To rail against God is to presume an *intrinsic Goodness* that our complaints against God implicitly betray. This *presumed Goodness* is the very 'God' who gives the lie to the god unbelievers reject.

Sin stems from our inability to sustain an 'intuition of being'.[128] Sin is a failure to appreciate 'the freshness deep down things'.[129]

Failing a sense of abiding amazement at the fortuity of existence, we are easily bored, and our actions become coarse and insensitive. Sin corrupts those who do not apprehend the 'mystery of being'.[130]

---

[128] See above, n. 56.

[129] *Gerard Manley Hopkins, God's Granduer.*

[130] Gabriel Marcel, *The Mystery of Being.*

The mystic is enamored of the 'intimate otherness' of things. The moralist, by contrast, is aggravated with imperfection. The saint is arrested by the sheer unexpectedness of things, whereas the religious cynic abhors surprises.

Stripped of political and religious legitimation, the logic of 'national identity' reveals itself as satanic and insane. Violence can never defeat violence, just as two wrongs never make a right. Didn't our mothers teach us that in 2nd grade?

No people can slaughter its way into security. That which we resist persists and grows in strength.

The 'myth of redemptive violence'[131] is as ubiquitous as it is illusory. 'How can Satan cast out Satan (Mk. 3:23)?'.[132] The enemy of my enemy is my friend ... until he's not.

Violence is both blind and addictive. Violence is an evil elixir that proves irresistible to those who know no better. At one time or another, that includes all of us (Lk. 23:34).

'Sin' is forgetfulness of being. 'Sin' is taking existence for granted. 'Sin' is a failure to appreciate the miracle of creation. Sin is a lack of gratitude for the gift of life.

---

[131] See above, n. 86.

[132] For a more nuanced and different interpretation, see René Girard, *I See Satan Fall Like Lightening*.

It is our desire for God, occluded by sin, that makes idolaters of us all. As easily as a child lured by the lollipop of a predator, we are persuaded to love a portion of the creation instead of the Creator.

Nothing in creation satiates our desire for divine Ecstasy. Ironically, it is our very desire for 'holy communion' that inspires us to find hook-ups that extinguish the ecstasy they promise.

In *ecstasy* did God create us, and for ecstasy did God configure us. Sin is the illusion that created objects or other persons can afford us the ecstasy we seek.

God is the tacit Source and Stimulus of our human yearnings, even those of unconscious complainers.

We must 'become like little children' to enter the kingdom of God (Lk. 18:17). Children grasp the gratuity of being better than adults.

Materialistic reductionism is *anathema* to the mystic. *Objectification* of anything, including the cosmos itself, is possible only by those ignorant of their own self-transcendence.

Discernment is more or less difficult depending on our degree of divinization. For those transfigured by God's Light in Presence, obedience is a matter of listening to the Spirit, not slavishly following rules and regulations.

The Paraclete comes to deliver us from religious torment. The rituals, rules and regulations of religion are children's play things for those illumined by the Divine Comforter (Jn. 14:16).

There is no sin God cannot forgive, no wrong God cannot right, no mistake God cannot correct. Hell is for those who remain incredulous at the prospect of universal salvation.

Opulence generates envy in the many, but *penthos* (tears of repentance) in the saint.

Evil arises through the pursuit of self-aggrandizement, is grounded in ignorance, and eventually results in murder.

Nothing prevents our deification more than contempt for its possibility. The kingdom of God is hidden from those who find the prospect of *theosis* preposterous.

Sin is not that we think too *much* of ourselves, or that we think of ourselves *too* much, but that we *think at all* without exercising 'presence of mind'.

Sin is less an act than an attitude. It's not what we *do* as sinners that grieves God so completely, but the *obtuseness* with which we stumble around in the darkness (Jn. 11:9).

What we say or do is something quite different from *how*, and to *what* purpose, we say or do it.[133] Sin is remaining either oblivious or indifferent to the unintended consequences of our words and actions.

Every form of reductionism is repugnant to those who experience their inherent self-transcendence. Materialism is incapable of its own justification.

Evil arises when human persons evade their inherent self-transcendence. The world is emptied of compassion when social engineering replaces self-transcendence as the impetus for change.

Every answer is always the beginning of another question. Conclusionary thinking is the corruption of culture. Without the curiosity of children, we are doomed to social decay.

There is no such thing as absolute emptiness. 'Nothingness' does not exist. We should reify evil no less than we should objectify God, though only God always 'is', whereas evil always 'is not'.

If God *wants* to save all but cannot, he is not omnipotent. If God *can* save all but doesn't want to, he is mendacious. If God *wants* to save all, *can* save all, and *does* save all, then he is a God worth believing in. If God doesn't want to save all, and cannot save all, then why call Him God?

---

[133] See John Searle, *Speech Acts: An Essay in the Philosophy of Language.*

Is it wrong to presume upon God's mercy? Only if we have not experienced the infinite depths of God's graciousness. Universal salvation is preposterous only for those whose God is too small.[134]

Why do many bristle at the prospect of universal salvation? Do they not mistake human freedom for irrational choice, and human responsibility for *hyper*-responsibility?

Is divine mercy constrained by human ignorance? Are those who reject universal salvation 'envious because God is so generous' (Mt. 20:15)?[135]

Belief in *Apokatastasis*[136] comes naturally to those who sustain a grateful astonishment at the mystery of existence. Failing this 'intuition of being', we find ourselves in 'the outer darkness where there is wailing and gnashing of teeth' (Mt. 25:30).

If Narcissus would have had the presence of mind to identify himself, not with what he saw in the water, but with the 'self' of the one casting his reflection, he would not have drown.

'Presence of mind' is the relativization of all thinking. 'Presence of mind' is no more reducible to cognition as cognition is to brain matter.

---

[134] J. B. Phillips, *Your God is Too Small.*

[135] For an entire book of such questions, see Philip Krill, *Aporiae: Inquiries from the Eschaton.*

[136] See above, n. 44.

How we do anything is how we do everything. Tigers never change their stripes. So too with God: 'We shall find God in everything alike, and find God always alike in everything'.[137]

Not realizing that human nature is inherently *ek-static*[138] is the main cause of the world's insanity. The failure to live consistently in self-transcendence is why there is so much suffering.

Imagine the hutzpah involved in developing a 'theological encyclopedia'! Mystically speaking, 'method' in theology is oxymoronic.

We are seldom aware of what we are *actually* doing when doing anything. Our motives are seldom what we think them to be. What we say we *want* to accomplish is often betrayed by the *way we go about* achieving it.

Knowing ourselves to be begotten by God (1 Jn. 5:1) and destined for joy,[139] it is natural for us to divest ourselves of all that is not of God. But what is not of God, save the insanity of our thinking in our ignorance of God?

---

[137] Meister Eckhart, quoted in James Geary, *Geary's Guide to the World's Great Aphorists*, 232.

[138] *'Ek-stasis'*, Greek (κστασις) for 'ecstasy', means 'to be or stand outside oneself'. It is used here to indicate that 'ecstasy' is the natural, automatic affective dimension to every act of self-transcendence ('standing outside oneself'). The fact that our consciousness is not self-enclosed but is teleologically oriented to open beyond itself, inclusive of all that exists, is also a participation in the God whose Presence-in-absence makes such self-transcendence possible.

[139] See above, n. 46.

CHAPTER SIX

Prayer

Contemplative prayer means abiding, with unrestricted openness and absence of analysis, in our *Vorgriff* of God. *Theosis* transpires in the space of 'naked intent'[140] towards God.

Contemplative prayer takes place in the epicenter of a heart empty of thoughts, yet filled with *divine longing*. Holy *desire* is what connects us with God.

A happy by-product of our *Vorgriff* of God is the awareness that our *desire* to know God *is* God, making us fruitful with his prevenient Presence.

---

[140] See above, n. 140.

Praying contemplatively means living from the *Le Point Vierge*[141] of our being. Contemplation is an *intentional foregoing of cognition* in exchange for an indistinct, but acute, openness to *That Which* we know not.

Humility overcomes the power of hubris, and hunkering down in God (through contemplative prayer) is the indestructible power that outlasts apocalyptic annihilation.

It's not that saints have no religious routines or rituals, but that they engage in them with enlightened indifference. They toggle unpredictably between 'naked intent'[142] towards God and overt expressions of denominational devotion.

Contemplative prayer is resting in our *Vorgriff* of God. Contemplative prayer is abiding with God in the 'deepest center'[143] of our souls.

---

[141] See above, n. 109.

[142] See above, n. 140.

[143] St. John of the Cross writes: 'O living flame of love, that tenderly wounds my soul in its ***deepest center!*** Since now You are not oppressive, now consummate ... tear through the veil of this sweet encounter!' (*Living Flame of Love*, Stanza 1, emphasis added). He also compares the *innermost recesses* of the heart to an 'inner wine cellar' where 'I drank of my Beloved...[and] no longer knew anything, and lost the herd which I was following'. He says, 'This wine cellar is the last and most intimate degree of love in which the soul can be placed in this life..[where] the seven gifts of the Holy Spirit are possessed perfectly...[and] [w]hat God communicates to the soul in this intimate union is totally beyond words' (*The Spiritual Canticle*, 26.1-4).

Mystics live in the 'Age (*Aeon*) to come' at every present moment. They apprehend a *Plērōma* of divine glory yet to come, while still inhabiting this present age.

Mystics live with the joyful trust that 'all will be well, and all manner of things will be well'.[144] They embody the Lord's admonition, 'Be not afraid' (Mt. 10:31; Lk. 12:32).

Saints experience 'the kingdom of God within' (Lk. 17:21), while also being intuitively aware of a cosmic consummation yet to be unveiled.

In alert, attentive, but mentally-empty silence, we experience the Presence of the unseen God. When attuned to 'absence' as another form of God's 'Presence', we 'attain, in an unspeakable and incomprehensible manner, a divine sweetness which surpasses word and mind'.[145]

If we abide intentionally, yet intuitively, in the 'Still Point'[146] of our being, we experience our deification taking place in real time. Simply by walking around 'feeling our feet' communicates a sense of being assimilated by the Infinite.

---

[144] Julian of Norwich, *Revelations of Divine Love*, Chapter 27.

[145] St. Maximus the Confessor, *Ambiguorum liber*, cited by Bulgakov, *ibid.*, 130.

[146] Phrase borrowed from T. S. Eliot, *Four Quartets 1: East Coker.*

'Be still and know that I am God' (Ps. 46:10). Or, as Meister Eckhart puts it, 'Do not prattle about God, for when you prattle about God, you are lying, you sin'.[147]

Interior surrender to God in the *Cloud of Unknowing*[148] is a participation in the *kenosis* of Christ (Phil. 2:6). The internal letting-go (*Gelassenheit*) of contemplative prayer is an epiphany of the risen Christ.

The *telos* (purpose, mission, goal) predestined for each of us by God is intuitively discovered as we enter more deeply into contemplative prayer. There, we encounter the One 'greater than ourselves' in whom, from whom, and to whom, 'we live and move and have our being' (Acts 17:28).

Our openness to the Infinite is a kind of *spiritual ovulation* that God alone can satisfy. Contemplative prayer is a virginal receptivity which attracts our Divine Spouse.

In contemplative prayer, we enter the 'inner room' where God, 'who sees in secret', meets us there 'in secret' (Mt. 6:6). Wordless and without thoughts, we gaze into the luminous darkness of the ungraspable God.

---

[147] Cited in: Graeme. ‚Meister Eckhart (Quotes) - Wisdom Trove'. *Wisdom Trove*, Nov. 2017.
[148] See above, n. 140.

In contemplative prayer, God touches us with a ray of his Light, which is darkness to the intellect but ecstasy to our spirits. Abiding in 'luminous darkness', we experience the ineffable Presence of God.

It's not a matter of 'going to heaven', but of *living there*. Heaven's not beyond the clouds, it's just beyond our fears'.[149] We live in 'hell' until we realize that 'the kingdom of God is within' (Lk. 17:21).

The distinction between 'nature and grace' is an accommodation for those unaware of their transcendental identity in God. In contemplative prayer, we acquire a co-natural knowledge of God in which such distinctions lose their meaning.

The Incarnation is both the source, and revelation of, humanity assimilated into the Life of God. In contemplative prayer, we experience the penetration and purification of our flesh by the Spirit of God.

Silence is the language of the Infinite. Only *that which* emerges unbidden and wordless from the fathomless depths of our being is worth saying or doing.

Silence is the 'Nothingness' in which we intuit a divine Totality. Silence is a space beyond polemics that promises the 'peace that passes all understanding' (Phil. 4:7).

---

[149] Garth Brooks, *Bellau Wood.*

In contemplative prayer, we become attuned to the 'small, still voice' (1 Kg. 19:12). In silence, we know by *unknowing*, and we begin to 'know as we are known' (1 Cor, 13:12).

Entering contemplation, we open ourselves to the No-thing-ness of God. Contemplation is the 'place of nowhere'[150] where we encounter the ineffable God.

God speaks in the innermost depths of our being. Contemplative prayer is laying ourselves open to interior revelations of God's hidden Self.

Contemplative prayer means abiding in that indefinable 'virginal point' of our being where our apprehension (*Vorgriff*) of the non-existent God takes place. Resting in *Le Point Vierge*,[151] we are inundated with Living Water, and, from this interior Garden, all fruitfulness comes forth.

Contemplative prayer is where we re-acquire the undefendedness of a child. In self-divestment, we remove our character armor,[152] allowing ourselves to emerge as the persons God knows us truly to be (cf. Col. 3:3; Rev. 2:17).

---

[150] See James Finley, *Merton's Place of Nowhere*.
[151] See above, n. 109.
[152] See Ernest Becker, *The Denial of Death*.

Eyes are the windows of the soul. Clear, soft eyes arise naturally from our unification with God in the still point[153] of our being.

All that is not of God must be dissolved if we are to blossom as the persons God desires us to be. The moment we alight upon our indissoluble unity with God in the virginal point of our being, this dissolution occurs of its own accord.

Nothing can be forced or coerced in our relationship with God. Sustaining a sense of our eternal, divinizing inclusion in God is the portal to perfect joy.

Religious rules and regulations, commands and ascetical practices, are for the purpose of making interior freedom possible. In contemplative prayer, religious 'formation' gives way to spiritual 'transformation'.

Contemplative prayer is like an interior 'Meeting Tent', which, after we enter like Moses to speak with God 'face-to-face', we emerge with countenances resplendent with divine Light (Ex. 34:35).

Contemplative prayer is an inner Mt. Tabor, where, in the Presence of the risen Christ, we are transfigured with the Father's uncreated Light.

---

[153] See above, n. 146.

Vorgriff

Contemplative prayer is described by Abba Lot, the desert father, who, when asked how we should pray, stood up, stretched his hands towards heaven, his fingers becoming like ten lamps of fire, and said, 'If you will, you can become all flame!'[154]

Self-surrendered union with God in the 'deepest center'[155] of our being releases, as from an interior point of Divine Life, a fluidity and relaxation that floods the body and overflows the soul.

Compassion comes naturally to those exercising *disponibilité*[156] towards God. Cultivating contemplative docility is the sum and substance of the spiritual life.

Contemplative prayer is an epiphany of God's self-communication. God Himself is the bliss-filled Origin and End of every act of contemplative Presence.

---

[154] *Joseph of Panephysis 6–7*. Found in: Lauren F. Winner, *Wearing God: Clothing, Laughter, Fire and Other Overlooked Ways of Meeting God*.

[155] See above, n. 143.

[156] *Disponibilité* means 'perfectly disposed to'. It is a term most often used to describe an actor's relationship to his or her role. As Hans Urs von Balthasar puts it, 'the actor's *disponibilité* for his role can be experienced psychologically in the most diverse ways, and this can lead to opposing theories. Many actors feel that they are (passively) 'in-dwelt' by the role, others feel that they (actively) 'inhabit' it; some experience particular emotions toward the role - or coming to them from the role. But as we have said, this does not bring about a split in consciousness; the actor's dedication to *his role will always be governed from a center of self-possession'* (*Theo-Drama, I*, 289-290, emphasis added).

GLOSSARY

Actus Purus (Pure Act) - the absolute Perfection of God; the unconditioned and ineffable Act of all acts, the Perfection of all perfections and the perfect Being of all created beings.

Advaita - a form of idealist monism, according to which the world has no separate existence apart from God [*Brahman*], the ultimate, transcendent and immanent Source of all that is.

Apophasis - a form of theological thinking which approaches God by way of negation. *Apophasis* was an important method of the early church fathers, and has greatly shaped the contemplative monastic tradition of the Eastern Orthodox Churches, as well as the mystical traditions of western Christianity.

Apokatastasis - Greek term referring to 'restoration'. *Apokatastasis* is prevalent among patristic era theologians regarding God's universally salvific, eschatological intentions for all creation, including that which was 'lost' through the Fall.

Apprehend - 'to grasp', 'to seize', 'to lay hold of'. In this book, *apprehend* refers to a pre-conceptual, intuitive way of 'knowing' God without any relation to our *ideas about* God.

Aseity - a technical term describing God's transcendence, God's completeness-in-Himself, so that all His acts and relations towards His people are based in grace, not necessity.

Atman - Sanskrit term for the innermost self or soul, often mistaken as separate from Brahman due to ignorance.

Aufhebung - a German term, found most notably in the writings of Hegel, which is often translated as 'sublation'. In its broadest sense, *sublation* describes the process of adopting a 'higher perspective' that preserves, negates, and perfects previous, more restrictive interpretive frameworks.

Brahman - Sanskrit synonym for 'God', i.e., the ultimate, all-encompassing reality that is eternal, unchanging, and beyond human perception.

Disponibilité - 'perfectly disposed to' - a term most often used to describe an actor's relationship to his or her role, used here to describe an interior 'availability' to an experience of God.

Efficacious Sign - a symbol that communicates what it signifies. This term is used in Catholicism to describe the symbolic power of the sacraments.

Ek-stasis - Greek (κστασις) meaning 'to be or stand outside oneself'. It is used here to indicate that 'ecstasy' is the natural, automatic affective dimension to every act of self-transcendence ('standing outside oneself).

Entelechy - a Greek term meaning the vital principle that guides the development and functioning of an organism or other system or organization.

Gelassenheit - a German word for 'tranquil submission', 'letting go', or 'divine releasement'. It is widespread in the Christian mystical tradition, especially as found in the writing of Meister Eckhart. See Philip Krill, *Gelassenheit: Day-by-Day with Meister Eckhart.*

Gnomic Will - Greek word meaning 'thought' or 'judgment', used in St Maximus in relation to volition; the 'deliberative' will in the sense of having to choose among competing options.

Inscape is an enigmatic concept about individuality and uniqueness derived by the poet Gerard Manley Hopkins from the ideas of the medieval philosopher John Duns Scotus. Hopkins uses the term *'Inscape'* to connote the distinctive design that constitutes individual identity.

Le Point Vierge - a phrase popularized by Thomas Merton to describe 'a point of nothingness at the center of our being which is untouched by sin and by illusion, a point of pure truth, a point or spark which belongs entirely to God, which is never at our disposal, from which God disposes of our lives … and is the pure glory of God in us'. Merton fastened on this concept by reading and corresponding with the Catholic Islamic scholar, Louis Massignon.

Light of Tabor - In Eastern Christian theology, *The Light of Tabor* is the light revealed on Mt. Tabor at the Transfiguration of Jesus. It is the uncreated, divine Light by which human beings are deified by the self-communication of God.

Logos/logoi – Greek terms with a wide range of meaning (given here in both singular and plural forms). The root of the English term 'logic' and of the suffix indicating categories of knowledge and study (biology, sociology, etc), *logos* was employed in the ancient world to describe the rationality informing the existence of all things. The plural *logoi* was used by Greek-speaking theologians to indicate the inner principle, essence, or intentionality behind all things, which in turn explains their natural participation or fellowship with the

Logos, who in Scripture is identified as none other than the Son of God Himself, the Father's agent of creation.

Noesis - the process of cognitive understanding or knowledge acquisition, particularly in the context of grasping abstract concepts or mystical truths.

Non Aliud - Latin term for 'not other'. Nicholas of Cusa (1401-1464) employs this phrase as an idiosyncratic 'name' for God in his efforts to formulate how God is both known and not known. *Non aliud* is a principle of thought associated with negative or apophatic theology.

Original Unity - a term coined by John Paul II to describe the human condition prior to the 'original sin' of Adam and Eve.

Pistis Christou - 'the faithfulness *of* Jesus Christ'. The ultimate meaning of 'salvation' is 'participation in' *pistis Christou*, i.e., in 'the faithfulness of Jesus Christ'.

Plērōma - Greek word translated 'fullness', or 'totality'. In Scripture (cf. Jn. 1:12-14; Eph. 1:22-23; Col. 1:19; 2:9-10), it refers to the fullness of God in Christ and the recapitulation and redemption of all things in Christ.

Reification - To reify something is to mistakenly attribute concrete existence to a transcendental phenomenon. This often happens with abstract ideas or predicates vis-a-vis God which are turned into independently existing things.

Sacchidānanda - a Hindu term that connotes the divine Bliss (*Ananda*) that arises within us when our Awareness (*Chit*) rests in Being (*Sat*), not in thinking.

Satori - a Japanese Buddhist term for 'awakening', 'comprehension', 'understanding', 'enlightenment'.

Shekhinah - an English transliteration of a Hebrew word meaning 'dwelling' or 'settling' and denotes the Presence of God. This concept is found in the Torah(Ex. 25:8)

Theandric - 'God human'. Theologically, *'theandric'* refers to those actions of Christ in which he used the human nature as an instrument of his divinity.

Totus Christus — Latin phrase meaning the 'whole Christ', and generally used in reference to the relationship between the Son of God and His Body, the Church, which together, bound in spiritual unity, constitute the Whole Christ. Rooted in the Trinitarian perception that even the Divine Persons are complete only in relation with each other, the doctrine of Totus Christus maintains that Jesus is complete only in relationship with His Body, the people He has won to Himself.

Ur-kenosis — In German, the prefix *ur* indicates an original or earliest form of something. *Ur-kenosis*, then, means the original or first instance of 'self-emptying', i.e., the self-emptying of the Father in the begetting of his Son, and of the Father and Son's mutual self-emptying in breathing forth the Holy Spirit.

Ur-sakrament - A phrase popularized by Karl Rahner to refer to Jesus Christ as the primordial sacrament of God's desire to give Himself completely to the whole of humanity.

Ur-sprung (German) - Source, Origin.

Ur-theophany - The premier revelation (manifestation) of God's ineffable Presence.

Vorgriff - German term used here to indicate an 'anticipatory grasp' of 'God' as an ineffable Mystery to which all human knowing and willing attains.

BIBLIOGRAPHY

Aristotle. 1976. *Posterior Analytics*. Cambridge, Mass.: Harvard University Press.

————. 1999. *Physics*. Oxford; New York: Oxford University Press.

Balthasar, Hans Urs von. 1994. *Theo-Drama Theological Dramatic Theory. Vol. IV, The Action*. San Francisco Ignatius Press.

————. 2010. *A Theological Anthropology*. Eugene, Or.: Wipf & Stock.

————. 2015a. *Theo-Drama: Theological Dramatic Theory / Volume I, Prolegomena*. Translated by Graham Harrison. San Francisco: Ignatius Press.

————. 2015b. *Theo-Drama: Theological Dramatic Theory / Volume V, The Last Act*. Translated by Graham Harrison. San Francisco: Ignatius Press.

Barron, Robert. 2016. *The Priority of Christ*. Baker Academic.

Becker, Ernest. 1997. *The Denial of Death*. New York: Simon & Schuster.

Behr, John. 2006. *The Mystery of Christ: Life in Death*. Crestwood, N.Y.: St. Vladimir's Seminary Press.

Benedict XVI, Pope. 2011. *Dogma and Preaching*. Ignatius Press.

Berlin, Isaiah. 1993. *The Magnus of the North: J. G. Hamann and the Origins of Modern Irrationalism*. Edited by Henry Hardy. New York: Farrar, Straus and Giroux.

Brooks, Garth. 1997. *Bellau Wood*.

Bulgakov, Sergius. 2013. *Unfading Light: Contemplations and Speculations*. Grand Rapids: Wm. B. Eerdmans Publishing Co.

Burrell, David B. 1993. *Freedom and Creation in Three Traditions*. University of Notre Dame Press.

Burrell, David B, Carlo Cogliati, Janet M Soskice, and William R Stoeger. 2010. *Creation and the God of Abraham*. Cambridge University Press.

Caussade, Jean Pierre, and Henri Ramière. 2011. *Abandonment to Divine Providence: [with Letters of Father de Caussade on the Practice of Self-Abandonment]*. San Francisco, Ca: Ignatius Press.

Chesterton, G.K. 2022. *Orthodoxy (Sea Harp Timeless Series)*. Destiny Image Publishers.

Covey, Stephen R. 1989. *The 7 Habits of Highly Effective People: Powerful Lessons in Personal Change*. New York: Fireside Press.

Creative Bloq Staff. '*Negative Space: 24 Brilliant Examples*'. Creative Bloq, 20 May 2019, www.creativebloq.com/art/art-negative-space-8133765.

Davison, Andrew. 2019. *Participation in God: A Study in Christian Doctrine and Metaphysics*. New York: Cambridge University Press.

Dunn, James D. G. 2008. *The Theology of Paul the Apostle*. Grand Rapids, Mich. Eerdmanns.

Eckhart, Meister. 2001. *Wandering Joy: Meister Eckhart's, Mystical Philosophy*. Edited and translated by Reiner Schürmann. Great Barrington, Ma: Lindisfarne Books.

———. 2014. *Meister Eckhart's Sermons*. Edited by Wyatt North. Wyatt North Publishing, LLC.

Eliot, T. S. 2014. *Four Quartets*. HarperCollins.

Geary, James. 2008. *Geary's Guide to the World's Great Aphorists*. Bloomsbury Publishing USA.

Girard, René. 2011. *I See Satan Fall Like Lightning*. New York Orbis Books.

Girard, René, Jean-Michel Oughourlian, and Guy Lefort. 2002. *Things Hidden Since the Foundation of the World*. Stanford, Calif.: Stanford University Press.

Girard, René, and Cynthia Haven. 2023. *All Desire Is a Desire for Being*. Random House.

Graeme. ,Meister Eckhart (Quotes) - Wisdom Trove'. *Wisdom Trove*, Nov. 2017, wisdomtrove.com/author_quotes/meister-eckhart-quotes/. Accessed 28 Oct. 2024.

Hamerton-Kelly, Robert. 1993.*The Gospel and the Sacred: Poetics of Violence in Mark*. Fortress Press.

Hart, David Bentley. 2009. *Atheist Delusions: The Christian Revolution and Its Fashionable Enemies*. Yale University Press.

———. David Bentley. 2013. *The Experience of God: Being, Consciousness, Bliss.* Yale University Press.

Harvey, Andrew. 2019. *Becoming God: 108 Epigrams from the Cherubinic Pilgrim by Angelus Silesius.* iUniverse.

Heschel, Abraham Joshua. 1954. *Man's Quest for God.* Macmillan Reference USA.

———. 1972. *God in Search of Man.* Octagon Press, Limited.

Hopkins, Gerard Manley. 1995. *'God's Grandeur' and Other Poems.* New York: Dover Publications.

John Paul, Pope. 2006. *Man and Woman He Created Them: A Theology of the Body.* Translated by Michael Waldstein. Pauline Books & Media.

Julian Of Norwich. 2015. *Revelations of Divine Love.* Oxford, United Kingdom: Oxford University Press.

Kimel, Alvin F. 2022. *Destined for Joy: The Gospel of Universal Salvation.*

Krill, Philip. 2022. *Mushin: Meditations on Mindfulness.* AuthorHouse.

———. 2023. *Aporiae: Inquiries from the Eschaton.* AuthorHouse.

———. 2024. *Ursprung.* AuthorHouse.

Kuhn, Thomas S. 2012. *The Structure of Scientific Revolutions.* Chicago: The University of Chicago Press.

Lawrence, Brother. 1967. *The Practice of the Presence of God.* Baker Books.

Lewis, C. S. 1995. *Surprised by Joy: The Shape of My Early Life*. New York; London: Harcourt Brace.

———. 2017. *Till We Have Faces: A Myth Retold*. HarperCollins.

Marcel, Gabriel. 2001. *The Mystery of Being*. South Bend, Ind.: St. Augustine's Press.

Maritain, Jacques. 1995. *Preface to Metaphysics*. Berkley.

Martin, Ralph. 2006. *The Fulfillment of All Desire: A Guidebook for the Journey to God Based on the Wisdom of the Saints*. Steubenville, Ohio: Emmaus Road Pub.

Mersch, S.J., Emile. 2018. *The Whole Christ: The Historical Development of the Mystical Body in Scripture and Tradition*. Translated by John R. Kelly, S.J. Ex Fontibus Company.

Merton, Thomas. 1968. *Conjectures of a Guilty Bystander*. Garden City, N.Y.: Image Books.

Milton, John, and Penguin. 2003. *Paradise Lost*. London: Penguin Books.

Nicholas of Cusa. 2024. *Nicholas of Cusa's on Learned Ignorance*. Edited by Karsten Harries. CUA Press.

Perl, Eric D. 2008. *Theophany the Neoplatonic Philosophy of Dionysius the Areopagite*. State Univ Of New York Pr.

Phillips, J. B. 2004. *Your God Is Too Small*. New York: Touchstone.

Plato. 2016. *The Republic of Plato*. Translated by Allan Bloom. New York Basic Books. (Orig. pub. 1968.).

Polanyi, Michael. 1966. *The Tacit Dimension*. Chicago, Ill: The University Of Chicago Press.

Rahner, Karl. 2001. *The Trinity*. London: Burns And Oates.

———. 2013. *Foundations of Christian Faith: An Introduction to the Idea of Christianity*. New York: Crossroad.

Rahner, Karl, Joseph F. Donceel, and Andrew Tallon. 1997. *Hearer of the Word Laying the Foundation for a Philosophy of Religion*. New York Continuum.

Russell, Norman. 2004. *The Doctrine of Deification in the Greek Patristic Tradition*. Oxford; New York: Oxford University Press.

Sanders, Fred. 2005. *The Image of the Immanent Trinity: Rahner's Rule and the Theological Interpretation of Scripture*. New York: P. Lang, Cop.

Sayers, Dorothy L. 2023. *The Mind of the Maker*. Alien Ebooks.

Searle, John Richard. 1969. *Speech Acts: An Essay in the Philosophy of Language*. Cambridge: Cambridge University Press.

Shea, Henry. 'Internal Difficulties in the Theology of Karl Rahner'. Modern Theology, vol. 37, no. 3, 27 Sept. 2020, https://doi.org/10.1111/moth.12652. Accessed 8 Jan. 2021.

Silesius, Angelus. 1986. *Angelus Silesius*. Paulist Press.

Spira, Rupert. 2017. *Being Aware of Being Aware*. Oxford: Sahaja, New Harbinger Publications.

St. Athanasius of Alexandria. 2011. *On the Incarnation / [I], Greek Original and English Translation*. Translated by John Behr. Yonkers, New York: St Vladimir's Seminary Press.

St. Augustine. 2009. *Confessions*. New York, NY: Classic Books America.

St. Bonaventure. 1953. *The Mind's Road to God*. Prentice Hall.

St. Irenaeus. 2010. *Against Heresies: The Complete English Translation from the First Volume of the Ante-Nicene Fathers / Monograph*. Edited by Alexander Roberts and James Donaldson. Ex Fontibus.

St. John of the Cross. 1991. *The Collected Works of Saint John of the Cross*. Translated by Kieran Kavanaugh, O.C.D. and Otilio Rodriguez, O.C.D. Washington: Institute Of Carmelite Studies.

St. Maximus the Confessor. 1985. *Maximus Confessor: Selected Writings*. Edited by George C. Berthold. New York: Paulist Press.

_____. n.d. *Ambigua Ad Johannem*.

St. Thomas Aquinas. 1981. *Summa Theologica*. Westminster: Christian Classics.

Sweet, William. 'Jacques Maritain (Stanford Encyclopedia of Philosophy)'. Stanford.edu, 2019, plato.stanford.edu/entries/maritain/.

Szarmach, Paul E. 1985. *Introduction to the Medieval Mystics of Europe*. State University of New York Press.

The Cloud of Unknowing: And the Book of Privy Counseling. 2012. The Doubleday Religious Publishing Group.

'The Reciprocity between Faith and Sacraments in the Sacramental Economy'. www.vatican.va/roman_curia/congregations/cfaith/cti_documents/rc_cti_20200303_reciprocita-fede-sacramenti_en.html.

Thunberg, Lars. 1995. *Microcosm and Mediator: The Theological Anthropology of Maximus the Confessor.* Open Court Publishing Company.

Tolle, Eckhart. 2010. *The Power of Now.* ReadHowYouWant.com.

Wikipedia Contributors. 2024. 'Koichi Tohei'. Wikipedia. Wikimedia Foundation. October 18, 2024. https://en.wikipedia.org/wiki/ Koichi_Tohei.

Winner, Lauren F. 2015. *Wearing God: Clothing, Laughter, Fire and Other Overlooked Ways of Meeting God,.* Harper Collins.

Wittgenstein, Ludwig. 1953. *Philosophical Investigations.* Oxford [U.A.] Wiley-Blackwell.

———. 1992. *Tractacus Logico-Philosophicus.* London; New York: Routledge.

Wright, N. T. 2013. *Pauline Perspectives: Essays on Paul, 1978-2013.* Minneapolis, MN: Fortress Press.

'You Are Not a Human Being Having a Spiritual Experience. You Are a Spiritual Being Having a Human Experience'. 2019. Quote Investigator. June 20, 2019. https://quoteinvestigator. com/2019/06/20/spiritual.

Zaretsky, Robert. 2021. ,Simone Weil's Radical Conception of Attention'. Literary Hub. March 9, 2021. https://lithub.com/ simone-weils-radical-conception-of-attention/.

Zizioulas, John D. 2010. *Communion and Otherness: Further Studies in Personhood and the Church.* Bloomsbury Publishing.

———. John D. 2004. *Being as Communion.* London: Darton Longman & Todd.

Printed in the United States
by Baker & Taylor Publisher Services